Gideon's Calling

The Founding and Development
of the
Schaghticoke Indian Community
at
Kent
Connecticut

1638-1854

James P. Lynch

HERITAGE BOOKS
2007

HERITAGE BOOKS
AN IMPRINT OF HERITAGE BOOKS, INC.

Books, CDs, and more—Worldwide

For our listing of thousands of titles see our website
at
www.HeritageBooks.com

Published 2007 by
HERITAGE BOOKS, INC.
Publishing Division
65 East Main Street
Westminster, Maryland 21157-5026

Other books by the author:

By "theire free act & deed"
Connecticut's Land Relationship with Indian Tribes, 1496-2003

International Standard Book Number: 978-0-7884-4248-1

Contents

Prologue

Who were the Schaghticoke Indians? Where did they come from? Were they native to the Kent, Connecticut area? Did they represent the amalgamation of many tribal remnants or were they the continuation of a single historical tribe?

The Schaghticoke Indians appeared as a result of historical occurrences at work both far and near. Schaghticoke was the product of two cultures in collision and its consequences. Schaghticoke as a community did not pre-exist the advent of continuous historical contact with Europeans but was created by it. This community had no one single source, it did not emerge from a single people. The origins and background of the people of Schaghticoke were legion. Schaghticoke represented a continuation not of a tribe or tribes, but of individuals' disrupted lives. Individuals who, for personal reasons we will never entirely know, sought shelter from the storm of change at "a bow in the river" at Gideon's calling.

This is their story.

Introduction

In September of 2005, the Bureau of Indian Affairs (BIA) issued what is called a *Reconsidered Final Determination* denying the Schaghticoke Tribal Nation of Connecticut the status of a federally recognized Indian tribe. Beneath the veneer of this decision was a tale of political intrigue, tens of millions of dollars in investment monies expended, accusations, counter-accusations, appeals, and reconsiderations by a besieged federal bureaucracy. The driving impetus for the Schaghticoke was Indian gaming. Back in 1988 Congress enacted the *Indian Gaming Regulatory Act* as a means of lifting Indian reservations out of abject poverty by allowing federally recognized Indian tribes, all 532 of them, to engage in gambling activities. The result was the advent of tribal-run casinos, in twenty-eight states from coast to coast.

The purported descendants of the colonial-era Schaghticoke Indian community also wanted their piece of this gaming action. In order to do so they had to leap through that flaming hoop known as the Federal Acknowledgment Process, FAP in short. This process consists of seven mandatory requirements that have to be met by a petitioning Indian group. Initially it appeared that Schaghticoke would succeed. The Bureau gave them a *positive* Final Determination. The Schaghticoke celebrated. Those opposing the decision yelled foul. The Bureau was found to have used incorrect procedures in analyzing critical information. They were also found to have used innovative non-regulatory criteria in order to bolster the Schaghticoke's faltering case. Most importantly, internal BIA e-mails revealed that Bureau researchers suppressed critical research that contradicted claims made by the Schaghticoke by simply not reading the research material supplied to them. Internal Bureau memoranda were uncovered wherein Bureau staff behind closed doors concluded that the Schaghticoke did not meet the critical requirements for recognition, continuous political authority and community through time. The memo went on to offer suggestions as to how to circumvent these mandatory criteria and recognize this petitioning group nevertheless. An appeal was made to the Interior

Board of Indian Appeals, an independent appellate agency within the Department of the Interior. The Bureau's positive determination was judged to be in error. The initial recognition determination was vacated by the Secretary of the Interior. The Bureau of Indian Affairs was instructed to reconsider the Schaghticoke decision, this time "going by the book." A *reconsidered* determination was made by the Bureau. The result: the Schaghticoke failed in their quest for riches.

Sadly, this is not the only such case. What gives this issue national importance is that across the United States other purported Indian or tribal petitioners are also seeking to cash in on this pot of gold called Indian gaming through the same federal organization. A federal agency, the Bureau of Indian Affairs remains favorably biased towards these gold seekers. It has the power to manipulate the criteria to make or break their quests. Of greater importance are the social, economic, and political impacts these corrupted decisions have on states and in communities surrounding these tribal petitioners. All this is political veneer. What ultimately wins out are the facts of the matter, that is, the hours of study performed by the historians, anthropologists, and genealogists who do the research, uncover the facts, and present them in a coherent fashion, understandable to the likes of lawyers, politicians, and federal bureaucrats. To them all, regardless of which side of the issue they are on, this writing is dedicated.

To begin, simply stated, the Schaghticoke failed on historical facts. They were not a tribe, never were. The historical facts presented in the following pages demonstrate they lacked that essential status of being an historical tribe since their first sustained historical contact with non-Indians. They lacked a second essential fact of not having a continuous autonomous tribal political leadership. This is that story.

My first involvement with the Schaghticoke was back in 1983. At that time, as a graduate student I was asked to assist the Schaghticoke in organizing and cataloging their historical and genealogical records in preparation for their recognition petition. During this time, on the basis of what I had seen at this early stage it was readily apparent that the Schaghticoke did not come together as a recognizable functioning Indian community until the advent of the

Moravian missionaries around 1749.[1] The passage of time has only reaffirmed those early conclusions.

Who were the Schaghticoke? Where did they come from? Were they native to the Kent, Connecticut area? Did they represent the amalgamation of many tribal remnants or were they the continuation of a single historical tribe? Were they ever a tribe in the historical sense? Question upon question, this has been the hallmark of investigations into this small Indian community that settled in the Berkshire foothills in the town of Kent, Connecticut. This is not the first attempt to answer these questions nor may it be the last.[2] What makes this effort different is that, unlike previous attempts, virtually all the historical information concerning this Indian community has been discovered and reviewed as a result of the present-day Schaghticoke Indians' quest for federal recognition as an Indian tribe.

We begin by establishing the historical context and setting within which the original Schaghticoke emerged. This setting geographically encompasses an area from Hudson's River east to Hartford, Connecticut and from Long Island Sound north following the Housatonic River valley to the Suffield-Stockbridge, Massachusetts area.

During the latter half of the seventeenth and first half of the eighteenth centuries, there existed within this area an extremely dynamic pattern of both socio-cultural and political change. On the one level, we find a dynamic political interplay and economic competition between the governments and colonists from three colonies (Massachusetts Bay, Plymouth, and Connecticut) and one province (New Netherlands/New York). The tension between them was one of competition for the lucrative Indian fur trade and also for land. Massachusetts Bay and New York were especially driven by their respective leaders' quest for fortune. Plymouth was driven by the need to pay off a massive debt owed to the company that financed their colony. A constant menace to all of them was the spectre of French intrusions into their respective colonies and provinces from Canada.

On another level, we find migrating colonists who, for the most part, were newcomers to this region, and, in some cases, to the continent. They fled the suffocating economic and social situations in their homeland of post-feudal England and the developing proprietary oligarchies in established colonial townships. In this process, they had to adapt the ways of the old world to that of the new. As the historian Colin Callaway noted, "People tend to construct their cultures in interaction with one another, not in isolation."[3] Change wrought by contacts between differing cultures is not one-sided. Each party continually modifies itself both in response to changing environmental settings, and in response to having to re-identify itself on the basis of encountering new cultures. Ethnicity is not a static concept. The English adapted to the presence of the Dutch and vice versa. The Indians of the region had to adapt to and live alongside not only both European cultures, but also to the ways of other tribes with whom they never previously had contact. All had to culturally adapt in various ways to one another. Within this cultural interplay there occurred the disruption of normative cultural and political patterns of the region's Indian tribes. As their respective societies encountered and adapted to the influx of remnants from displaced or dispersed Indian tribes, they too had to adapt. Indian culture was not monolithic. Different tribes came from different cultural traditions. Each may have found the other strange. Kinship, social status, political leadership, oral traditions, marriage patterns, and environmental exploitation strategies varied among each. Tribes as corporate bodies were only able to adapt to such encounters to a limited degree, and only as long as their own cultural setting was not severely disrupted. But this was not to be the case.

A third level represents the cultural, economic, and political interplay between the Indians and the advancing colonists. Traditionally, New England Indian tribes were seasonally sedentary within recognized tribal lands. Oftentimes villages within these territories moved to different locations within their established territory on the basis of a seasonally-based subsistence cycle. Based on these seasonal movements, early colonial observers incorrectly deducted that New England tribes lacked fixed abodes. Both sides were adapting to new environmental situations and trying to understand one another. Mistakes and misjudgments were made on both sides. Yet the learning curve was continually rising. Many Indian individuals showed remarkable ingenuity in adapting to the new realities of this encounter. There were some Indians who became quite proficient linguists, speaking English, Dutch, French, and German. Some colonists were accused of "going Indian." Somewhere within this matrix of change we will find the Schaghticoke, their origins, and community development through time.

We will also find that the community at Schaghticoke represented a microcosm of this process of change at work. As socio-cultural change is not a static concept, so too were not the Schaghticoke. The story of this community is one of evolution. The Schaghticoke community of 1741 bore little resemblance to the community of 1853. As a result, this research reaches beyond the founding of the community at Schaghticoke and also focuses upon the development of the community from its inception to 1854, perhaps the high point in its economic and social development. It will examine factors that both inhibited and facilitated the political, social, and economic emergence, decline and reemergence of this state reservation-based community. It will show why they never became nor ever will be federally recognized as an Indian tribe.

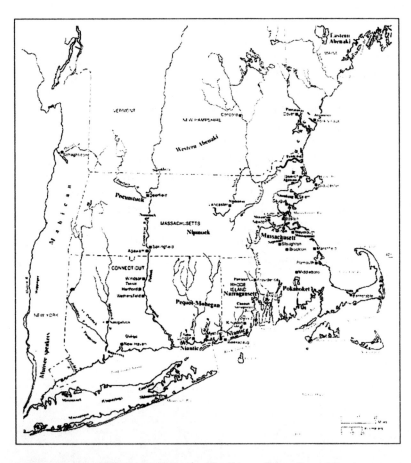

Map 1. Adapted from B. Salwen, "Indians of Southern New
England: Early Period," in *Handbook of North American Indians*,
Volume 15. Smithsonian Institute, 1978.

Chapter One

Avenues and Displacement

As has oftentimes been the case in history, incidents that happened during different years and many miles apart have consequences that even the greatest of sages cannot foretell. Schaghticoke, as we shall see, was one such manifestation and consequence of seemingly unrelated occurrences.

The first incident occurred in the Dutch colony of New Netherlands. In Europe at this time, the Netherlands were a loose confederation of provinces or states led by an elected state's general. Exploration on the behalf of these confederated states was conducted by state-chartered companies. The Dutch had two: the Dutch East India Company and the Dutch West India Company. The West India Company contracted the services of an English sea captain named Henry (Henrick) Hudson. He was hired to explore and discover an ice-free sea passage to ports in Russia for trade. Failing this adventure, he headed west, encountering the east coast of America. In September of 1609, Hudson discovered and explored the river and estuary that were to bear his name, Hudson's River. The Dutch States General laid claim to the lands adjacent to this river by virtue of Hudson's discovery. They named this land New Netherlands. By virtue of a charter from the States General, in 1623 the Dutch West India Company established a company-run trading settlement there named New Amsterdam. During the summer of 1623, the ship *New Netherland*, flying the flag of the Dutch West India Company, ventured up Hudson's River carrying eighteen Dutch families. *New Netherland* deposited her passengers "on the west shore of the river just above Castle Island"[1] near present-day Albany. Under the direction of Adriaen Joris, these settlers founded the trading post, Fort Orange. Later, after the British conquest of the Dutch forces at New Amsterdam (New York City) this fur-trading center became known as Fort Albany. One part of the Schaghticoke puzzle came into play. These first settlers reported that soon after their settling at Fort Orange, Indians from at least six surrounding tribes came to trade furs with them. They noted that the Indians "were as quiet as lambs, and came and traded with all the freedom imaginable."[2] Fort Albany also became a point of entry for colonial settlement of the fertile lands that lay to its east, across Hudson's River.

In 1636, William Pynchon, a Massachusetts fur trader and business partner of Massachusetts Bay Governor John Winthrop (the elder) purchased lands near the Connecticut River from the Agawam Indians. Pynchon's and Winthrop's purpose was to establish a fur trade with Indians to the west and those along the north-reaching Connecticut River Valley. By doing so, they would break the near monopoly on this lucrative trade dominated by their competitors, the Pilgrims of Plymouth Colony.[3] The lands they purchased lay astride the main Indian path (known to the colonists as the "Bay Path") running from the Narragansett and Pequot country in southwest Connecticut and Rhode Island to the lands of the Mohawk in eastern New York, terminating not too distant from the Dutch at Fort Orange.[4] Pynchon's trading post eventually became Springfield, Massachusetts. Pynchon's settlement soon opened the door for trade with the Indians in western and northern Massachusetts. It also became a portal for colonial settlement into the very heart of this western region of the colony.

One year after the founding of Pynchon's trading post in 1637, following the rout of the Pequot Indians at Mystic, Connecticut by a mixed colonist-Indian force under Captain John Mason, a segment of remnant Pequot fled west along the Connecticut coastline towards the Dutch colony of New Netherlands. This remnant was trapped in a swamp in present-day Southport, Connecticut by the pursuing colonial and Indian forces.[5] The resulting battle became known as the "Swamp Fight." Aiding this trapped remnant Pequot group in resisting the colonial forces was a neighboring tribe, the Pequannock.[6] The Pequot and Pequannock were defeated. Most either were killed in the fight or were taken captive. A number of the Pequot and Pequannock were able to avoid capture or surrender and fled northwest towards the country of the Mahican tribe who resided to the north and east of Fort Orange.

As a result of this military success, the colony of Connecticut claimed by right of conquest all those lands west of the Connecticut

River to the present-day Norwalk River in western Connecticut.[7] These appropriated lands included all the tribal territories belonging to the Pequannock Indians. To the victor go the spoils. The net result of not only this incident, but those of the Dutch presence at Fort Orange, and Pynchon's settlement in Massachusetts, was to open the region up for colonial settlement and to set in motion an Indian displacement process that led to the establishment of an Indian settlement at a place along the Housatonic River the Mahican tribe called *Schaghticoke* ("where two rivers meet").

The Housatonic River winds its way south from Vermont and empties into Long Island Sound at present-day Stratford, Connecticut. From this southern terminus, a trail ran north following the Housatonic up to present-day Sheffield (Westenhook), Massachusetts. Along its length, this trail also bisected the east-west Narragansett-Mohawk (Bay Path) trail that ran past William Pynchon's trading post. Numerous branch trails also existed that linked numerous regional Indian villages and settlements to one another. One of these trails that ran east from New York terminated on the Housatonic River. It was to become the site of Schaghticoke.

As colonial expansion accelerated, these trails served not only as avenues of ingress by the colonists into tribal territories, but they also served as arteries of egress by displaced tribal fragments out of their former territories. They were the victims of the collision of two differing cultures, ideologies, economic systems, and armed conflict. Along these numerous avenues of egress, expatriate Indian villages consisting of tribal remnants developed. Among them were two, Schaghticoke (New York) and Stockbridge (Massachusetts). As we shall see, a third was to emerge.

War,[8] territorial loss due to land conveyances, and epidemics were the principal catalysts for these displacements. Some of these remnants joined missionary-owned "Praying Towns" in an effort to adapt to English culture. Many fled simply to preserve their cultural norms. Among these westward-fleeing refugees were those from tribes formerly resident in Rhode Island, eastern Massachusetts, and Connecticut. During this journey some of these refugees turned north at the Connecticut River, joining up with the northern tribes such as the Abenaki. Others continued on west, seeking refuge among the Mahican tribe (who in turn were gradually being pushed eastwards due to the establishment of colonial settlements out of Albany) or westward among the Five Nation Iroquois, most notably among the Oneida tribe.[9] Many of these refugees also settled at the expatriate Indian village of Schaghticoke on Hudson's River near Albany. This village was established by the English[10] authorities in 1677 as a refuge for such fleeing remnants. The English authorities at Albany were fearful that these tribal remnants would join up with French-allied Indian tribes such as the Canadian Abenaki of St. Francis, a notoriously pro-French tribe. This expatriate village was placed under the control of a Mahican tribal sachem. Beginning in 1734, other refugees settled at the Indian mission established by the Reverend John Sergeant (formerly of Springfield) at Stockbridge, Massachusetts. But as we shall see, these were not the only gathering locations for displaced Indians.

The advent of this east-west out-migration of displaced Indians and tribal remnants represented only a part of the process of tribal disintegration and dispersal that was occurring in the region. Beginning in 1638, occurrences to the south, at the mouth of the Housatonic River, were to give further impetus to a second migration that began in the aftermath of the 1637 Swamp Fight.

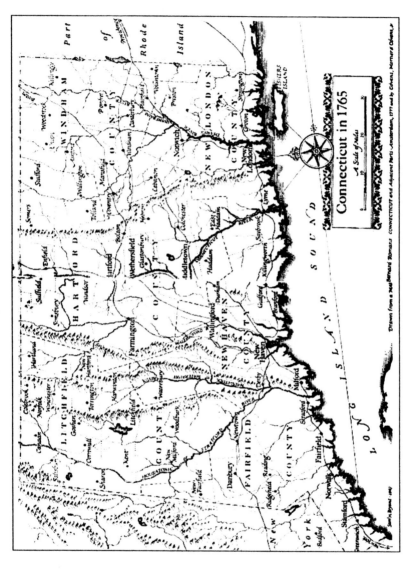

Map 2. Connecticut in 1765. Library of Congress Map Division.

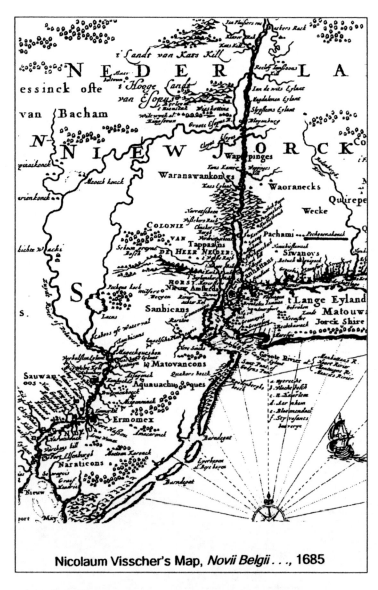

Nicolaum Visscher's Map, *Novii Belgii . . .*, 1685

Map 3. The "Waoranecks" cited on this map are the
Weantinock/Potatuck. The "Quirepy's" are the Paugussett
tribe. The "Pechquenaknock" are Pequannock tribe.
Library of Congress, Map Division.

Chapter Two

Colonial Settlements and the Housatonic River Tribes

Aftermath

Up to this point, we have seen Indian tribes located in northern Connecticut and Massachusetts being squeezed westwards towards New York. At the same time, Indian tribes such as the Mahican, who resided to the east of Albany, were being pressured eastward towards Connecticut. The French and Abenaki to the north served to deter large-scale tribal migrations in that direction. Our attention now looks to the south, to the mouth of the Housatonic River.

Two immediate consequences appeared in the aftermath of the 1637 Swamp Fight. First, a tribe, the Pequannock, having suffered military defeat by colonial forces, saw their lands being lawfully taken by the colony of Connecticut. The colony did so by right of conquest.[1] By this lawful seizure, all Indian or native right to these lands was forfeited to Connecticut. The Pequannock acknowledged this act in a May 25, 1671 confirmatory deed.[2] Second, these rich and bountiful former tribal lands became open to colonial settlement.

Those Pequannock who chose to remain were restricted by the Connecticut General Court of Elections to two village sites, one at Uncowa (in present-day Bridgeport) and one at Sasgua (in present-day Fairfield). In 1659, in response to the settlement of two towns (Stratford in 1639 and Fairfield in 1640), the Connecticut General Court of Elections further ordered that eighty acres of proprietary common land be set aside for the conditional use as a reservation for the remnant Pequannock.[3] This tract of land became known as the Golden Hill reserve. By 1725 only forty Indians remained.[4] The reserve was abandoned by 1738.

The year following the Swamp Fight (1638) brought the establishment of a proprietary plantation[5] at Milford by colonists from New Haven colony. Milford was situated on the eastern side of the Housatonic River estuary. These lands were occupied by the Paugussett tribe.[6] The Paugussetts' tribal lands spanned both sides of the lower Housatonic River. The Paugussett were not participants in the 1637 Swamp Fight and therefore were not considered belligerents by the colony. As a result the Milford proprietors in the process of founding a plantation there had to obtain deeds of conveyance of native right (or occupancy right) from the Paugussett tribal leadership.[7] Eventually, having conveyed their lands in Milford, the remnant Paugussett were settled on a 100-acre reservation at Turkey Hill.[8] By 1725, forty-nine Indians remained there.[9]

The following year (1639), Stratford (originally Cupeag) plantation was settled by colonists from Newton, Massachusetts. They left the Massachusetts Bay Colony with the permission of the Massachusetts General Court to establish a settlement with more arable lands and to establish their own church. Stratford lay opposite Milford on the Housatonic River's west bank. Stratford's land grant encompassed both Pequannock and Paugussett tribal lands. The settlement bordered Fairfield on the west and Milford to her east. Her grant encompassed lands twelve miles inland from Long Island Sound. Former Pequannock tribal lands that lay within Stratford's land grant did not need to be obtained from the Indians. Those that were on Paugussett lands did. By 1680, all the Paugussett tribal lands within Stratford were lawfully obtained by the town proprietors. The remnant of the Paugussett tribe in Stratford was settled on a 100-acre reservation known as the Coram Hill reserve.[10]

Fairfield, bordering west of Stratford, was also settled by Massachusetts colonists in 1640. This grant encompassed all former Pequannock tribal territory. As noted earlier, the Pequannock remnants were settled on the Golden Hill reserve in 1659.

Derby, whose west boundary was upon the Housatonic River, was to the north of Stratford. It was settled in 1655 on former Paugussett tribal lands. The remnant of the Paugussett joined those on the Turkey Hill reservation in Milford. Others moved upriver.

Further up the Housatonic was the plantation of Woodbury. It was settled by religious dissidents from Stratford in 1674. Woodbury at the time of settlement contained a major Indian village

(Potatuck) belonging to the Potatuck tribe. By 1725, fifty Indians remained in the town.[11]

New Milford, which bordered north on Woodbury was settled in 1706. This settlement also contained a second Potatuck village called Weantinock. In 1725, there remained forty-nine Indians in New Milford.[12] It also encompassed a third Potatuck settlement adjacent to the "Great Falls," three miles downriver from Weantinock and two miles upriver from the Potatuck village in Woodbury. These last two named towns (Woodbury and New Milford) would have a major effect upon the upper Housatonic River Indian tribes and the establishment of an Indian settlement at Schaghticoke.

These upper river tribes were mentioned by Connecticut Governor Joseph Talcott in his detailed correspondence regarding Indians remaining within the colony. In this September 30, 1725 correspondence, he mentioned two other Indian settlements north of New Milford along the Housatonic River in "ye North Wt. Corner of this Coloney," Weataug, containing about fifty Indians, and ten miles further north an Indian settlement he referred to as "Owseetumac" (Housatonic, located in present-day Sheffield, Massachusetts), containing an Indian population of "about 30."[13] As we shall see, these two villages belonged to the Mahican tribe. Of even more importance, Governor Talcott made no mention of any Indians residing on the Housatonic River at a place called Schaghticoke circa 1725. Why? There was none.

This is the historical setting in which Schaghticoke emerged. The region had become boxed in by colonial expansion and settlement. The Indian population of the region was being compressed. Adding to this pressure were those expatriate Indians moving westward through this area. These tribal remnants, the product of tribal disintegration and fissioning, were seeking refuge from this storm of change. Their condition was worsened by the presence of so many differing tribal remnants representing dissimilar social norms. What were the consequences of this process in the region under our study?

Chapter Three

Displacement and Fragmentation

The Lower Housatonic River Valley Tribes

What happened to the main portion of the Pequannock and Paugussett Indian populations? These Indian tribes of the lower Housatonic River Valley were culturally similar though they may have varied in form of political leadership.

During an eighty-six year period (1639-1725), tribal political leadership failed and ageless lineage structures collapsed. Individuals and families left the area not as coherent social groups but as fragments. This displacement process was accelerated, as we have seen, by the continual establishment of numerous northward-reaching proprietary plantations along the Housatonic River Valley. No wars occurred between settlers and tribes in this region. It was simply cultural displacement. One group's social, ideological and economic strategies simply could not continue in the face of large-scale loss of land. On the other hand, with the purchase and consolidation of every new acre of land, colonial political and economic dominance increased. One culture could not adapt to change; the other drew strength from it.

The net result of this displacement process was that by the advent of the eighteenth century the two principal tribes of the lower Housatonic Valley, the Pequannock and Paugussett, had dispersed, save only two remnant groups at the Golden Hill (Pequannock) and at the Coram Hill and Turkey Hill (Paugussett) reservations. The majority of the two tribes' populations fragmented and dispersed either westward, joining the Hudson's River Valley *Wappinger* tribe, or northward, among the Potatuck and Mahican tribes; while some settled among the *Tunxis* tribe in the Farmington, Connecticut area. Some of these refugees eventually joined the Christian Indian community at Stockbridge, Massachusetts.[1]

By 1740 Stockbridge had an Indian population of 120 Christian converts[2] which included a significant number of *Wyachtonok* (Weantinock-Potatuck) Indians and "a sprinkling of other

Connecticut Tribes."[3] By 1743, this number increased to 218. This population included 125 baptized Indians. Of these baptized, forty-two were actual church communicants.[4] Still others moved westward, settling among the Oneida Iroquois. This process was to repeat itself, this time upon the Potatuck tribe.

The Potatuck of the Mid-Housatonic River Valley

The Potatuck were the rock that sat in the middle of the Housatonic River. Their political importance to the region was substantial. Their principal village at Potatuck was the site of important regional intra-tribal meetings. Their tribal lands extended from the Town of Derby, Connecticut, north to the Massachusetts border. The historical record depicts them as a peaceable tribe. There are no known instances of their engaging in conflicts with neighboring tribes or with the colony of Connecticut. When this rock shattered under the pressure of colonial expansion, the dynamics of change in this region accelerated. The Mahican tribe that bordered Potatuck tribal territory on the west and north, already under colonial acculturative pressure from the east, now suddenly had their southern and eastern flanks laid bare when the rock in the Housatonic gave way. What happened?

The first possible sustained contact with the Indians of the mid-Housatonic River Valley was in 1642. Stephen Goodyear, a proprietor of New Haven Colony, established a trading house at Derby at the confluence of the Housatonic and Naugatuck rivers.[5] According to tradition, Goodyear then established a second trading post up the Housatonic River on an island which bears his name sometime between 1642-1646. This island was just to the south of the Indian village at Potatuck. Additionally in 1663, the Dutch authorities at Fort Orange (Albany) became aware of the existence of "another tribe of Indians that dwell halfway between Fort Orange and Hartford..."[6] The Dutch had become aware of the Potatuck. When the Moravian missionaries from Pennsylvania first arrived among the Mahican tribal villages in the late 1730s they heard the Mahican speaking of the *Wampano (wa panwi: it dawns)*[7] people or "eastern people." These missionaries, being of German origin, heard this term with their native ear and Germanized *Wampano* into

Wompanach. They applied it as a generic reference to the Housatonic River Valley Indian peoples to the east of the Mahican village of Shecomeko where they first resided. The Moravians identified these Wompanach as such in contrast to other neighboring Indian groups such as: *Mahik, Esopus, Hooglanders* (uplanders), and *Potatik.*

Among these Wompanach peoples were the *Potatik.* This was the Moravian/German dialectical rendering of Potatuck. *Potatik* referred to the Potatuck tribe. The Dutch and English authorities in neighboring New York also referred to the Potatuck as the *Wawyachtenokse* or *Wawyachtenok*[8] (literally, people of where the river bends) an apparent Dutch/Mahican rendering of the Mahican *Weantinock,* the geographical location of the Potatuck village in New Milford which was situated on a field (known as Indian Field) upon a pronounced river bend.

By 1668, colonists moving up the Housatonic River from Stratford were making land purchases from this Potatuck tribe. These Potatuck were led by their tribal sagamore *Atterosse.* Also present was *Chesusumock.* He was the village sachem or chief of the tribe's namesake village, Potatuck. This village was located at the confluence of the Housatonic and Pomperauge rivers in present-day Southbury, Connecticut. The early Woodbury land documents, 1668-1670, involved land conveyances associated with lineages of this tribal village.

The Potatuck tribe[9] maintained a centralized political authority. Tribal leaders emerged from their main villages (Weantinock and Potatuck). The Potatuck also maintained a tribal political structure similar to that of the historic Paugussett tribe to their south. This political structure was led by a tribal sagamore and subordinate village sachems that in turn represented village lineages. The presence of a tribal sagamore among the Potatuck was confirmed in 1720:

> It is resolved, That Capt. John Sherman of Woodbury, and Major John Burr of Fairfield, taking with them Thomas Minor of Woodbury, or such other interpreter as they shall judge meet, do repair immediately to the said Indians at Po-ta-tuck and Wi-an-ti-nuck, and cause the said Chickens, to

whom the said belts and wampum were sent, to attend them, and make the best enquiry they can into the truth of the said story, and what may be the design of such message; and as they shall see cause, take proper order that said Indian with the belts, *and the principal or chief of the Potatuck and Wiantinuck Indians,* attend the general Court at their next sessions....[emphasis added][10]

There is no evidence that tribal leadership titles as a policy were inherited. Tribal sagamores appeared to have emerged from both villages (Potatuck and Weantinock). Senior leadership roles appeared to have been achieved rather than being ascribed by lineage affiliation. Age and social/political standing appeared to have been major criteria. There was also a Potatuck village at the Great Falls south of Weantinock. It was not as large as Potatuck and Weantinock nor was the topography suitable for extensive agriculture. But it became a politically important location. *Wereamaug,* from the village of Weantinock (he was village sachem circa 1716), who later became the tribe's sagamore, made his residence there until his death in 1722. Both Potatuck and Weantinock were typical sedentary riverine villages that extensively engaged in agriculture. The tribe's numerous sub-settlements scattered throughout its traditional territory appeared to be seasonal.

According to one document a third village, *Kenunckpacooke,* was reputed to be located to the north of Weantinock on the east side of the Housatonic River. It was mentioned in the Benjamin Fairweather deed of June 1716 as being led by a sachem called *Nepato.*[11]

The historic territory of the Potatuck tribe was vast. There were many sub-settlements scattered throughout their territory. The lands of the Potatuck covered the present-day Connecticut towns of Southbury, northwest Derby, Oxford, Woodbury, western Middlebury, New Milford, New Fairfield, Warren, Washington, west Litchfield and south Kent and the lands on the east side of the Housatonic River up to the present Connecticut-Massachusetts state line. The parameters of Potatuck tribal territory were defined by an analysis of land conveyances made by identifiable Potatuck leaders. (See Appendix A.)

By April of 1671,[12] lands were being conveyed by Potatuck Indians associated with the northern village at Weantinock. Weantinock was located on the west side of the Housatonic River across from the present center of New Milford. At the time of first contact, this village was led by sachem named *Pocono*. He was succeeded by *Pinawee* (also known as *Papetopo* or *Pompkinseds*). By 1705 the majority of lands lying within the town of Woodbury and those within New Milford, including the site of the village of Weantinock, had been conveyed to the colonists.[13] Lands remaining to the tribe included those surrounding the village of Potatuck, lands of a third unnamed village immediately adjacent to the Great Falls on the west bank of the Housatonic, midway between Weantinock and Potatuck, and those lands to the north and east of Woodbury.

Individuals from disintegrated tribes were also present among the Potatuck. They were from the former Paugussett, Pequannock, and possibly the Quinnipiac tribes. In their records the Moravians identified and referred to these expatriate individuals as Wompanach as opposed to Potatik.

Potatuck Diaspora

The dispersal of the Potatuck tribe coincided with the establishment of the plantation at Woodbury in 1674. As the lands surrounding their village were conveyed to proprietary committees from nearby Woodbury plantation (1683-1701), the movement of Potatuck individuals and families out of the village of Potatuck increased, though as we will see, this particularly important tribal village remained politically and socially intact until 1758.

As a reflection of the impact of cultural contact, as early as 1686 three Potatuck sachems petitioned the English magistrates at Albany for permission to leave their tribal lands in Connecticut and join their New York "brethren...the Indians of Tachkanik."[14] Permission was granted. With the establishment of New Milford plantation in 1702 and the subsequent land conveyances by the tribe (1702-1705), population dispersal from the nearby Potatuck village of Weantinock began in earnest. The Indian Field site of the village of Weantinock was conveyed to the New Milford proprietors in 1705.[15]

Evidence of Potatuck population dispersal and decline can be extrapolated from the historical record, which demonstrates that the dispersal of a major portion of the Potatuck population occurred prior to any mention of a settlement at Schaghticoke. In 1703, John Minor of Woodbury, a gifted linguist and colony interpreter, undertook a census of adult males of the Indian tribes in the region.[16] Besides surveying the two Potatuck villages he also surveyed the "Indians belonging to N. Haven & Brandford," "Darbee Indians," and "Paquannuck Indians." Minor's report made no reference to any Indian village existing at Schaghticoke.

At each of the two Potatuck villages, Minor enumerated nineteen adult males. (See Appendix C.) A gross estimate based upon the number of adult males enumerated by Minor times four, would give each village a conservative population estimate of around seventy-six individuals or a total tribal membership of approximately one hundred and fifty-two people.

In 1725, Governor Talcott's survey[17] of the Potatuck Indian population was given at ninety-nine:

> ...The oweantanag Indians, fourty and Nine live in New-milford, on ye West Side of the sd town...In Woodbury about fifty live about 3 miles from sd town....

Given that the village site of Weantinock was conveyed to New Milford in 1705, this New Milford Indian population must have been those residing at the Great Falls. This number represents a population decrease of approximately fifty-three persons over a twenty-two-year period.

A 1742 petition (memorial) to the Connecticut General Assembly[18] noted that there remained thirty Potatuck at the Great Falls in New Milford and forty at the village of Potatuck, or a total Potatuck population of seventy, a decrease of twenty-nine people over a seventeen-year period.

From 1703 to 1725 the Potatuck tribal population decreased by an estimated fifty-three people. From 1725 through 1742, the estimated population decrease was twenty-nine. The total estimated population decrease from 1703-1742, a period of thirty-nine years, was ninety-two. Most important was the steep decline between 1705 and 1725, which amounted to just under forty percent of the estimated 1705 population.

Where did these people go? Unlike Massachusetts and New York, there were no reported outbreaks of epidemics in western Connecticut during this period. The avenues of egress from these village locations was not only upriver towards the Massachusetts Mahican villages located at Housatonic (Scatacook) and later Stockbridge, but also to the northwest including the New York Indian villages at Shecomeko, Schaghticoke (New York) and as we have noted earlier, Takonic. Some may have also joined the St. Francis Abenaki in Canada.

Evidence of an early population movement out of Weantinock prior to the 1705 sale is found in a deed recorded in Woodbury, Connecticut.[19] In this 1704 deed of sale to a group of Potatucks for lands in Armenia, New York, the following is noted:

> ...a tract of 7,500 acres near Armenia and Wassaic which ran to a high mountain called Weeputting Mountain, then southwesterly along the ridge of a mountain..." by Richard Sackett

> Wusumpe Tamquash Yong-sing-pom-kin-feet (aka Papetopo, Pompkinseds, sachem of Weantinock) Occumbus Wyawaw and Younghan's squaw on behalf of her sons.

What is important to note is that the village sachem of Weantinock along with other village members were at this point in time migrating out of the area and adopting the English practice of purchasing land. From 1705 on, their names disappeared from the historical record.

Potatuck Persistence

By 1705, the majority of lands lying within both the towns of Woodbury and New Milford had been conveyed by the Potatuck. These conveyances included the site of the village of Weantinock. The lands remaining to the tribe were those surrounding the village of Potatuck, lands immediately adjacent to the Great Falls, and those to the north and east of Woodbury. The village at Potatuck

remained as an Indian settlement until 1758 when the last of their
lands were conveyed to the town of Woodbury.

Furthermore, a series of Potatuck land conveyance deeds
between 1705 and 1734 (the last of the Potatuck land conveyances
until the final village land sales in 1758) demonstrates a continuum
of Potatuck tribal political activity:

October 25, 1705 - Third Kettletown Purchase
May 28, 1706 - Woodbury Confirmatory Deed
July 25, 1706 - Newtown Purchase
January 31, 1710 - Little River Purchase
March 2, 1715 - Litchfield/Bantam Purchase
June 19, 1716 - Fairweather Purchase
October 22, 1720 - Hartford/Windsor Purchase
June 23,1722 - Wereamaug's Quit claim
August 7, 1723 - Second Newtown Purchase
March 6, 1728 - Promiseck Purchase
August 1, 1733 - Cockshure Field Conveyance
January 24, 1733 - South Purchase
January 18, 1734 - South Purchase II

These deeds conclusively show that despite the 1705 sale of
Weantinock, the Potatuck tribe continued to function as a socio-
political tribal entity through 1734. From that year forward the
primary source documentation supports the continued existence of
the tribe through 1758, long after the advent of an Indian
community and political organization at Schaghticoke. The evidence
shows the continued close social relationship between the Potatuck
settlements at Potatuck and the Great Falls in the period after the
sale of Weantinock. As an example, in the fall of 1722 Wereamaug
(*Weromaug*), the Potatuck sagamore, took ill with consumption. In
trying to combat his illness, Wereamaug's wife asked for the
assistance of *Womsuckaway,* the shaman of Potatuck village, to
conduct a *pow wow* to cure the fatally ill sagamore.[20]

Additionally, in the February 22-April 9, 1742 journal of the
Moravian missionaries Gottlob and Buttner,[21] they noted that they
sent one of their converts (John-Johannes, a Mahican) "...to
Potatick, to tell the Indians there...something of our savior...."
They also noted some "...Indians came from Potatick...." The

Potatuck also requested that a Moravian missionary be sent to them. This document showed that a functioning Indian community was still present at Potatuck circa 1742. It also represented a concerted community-based effort to obtain a Moravian missionary.

A May 1742 Memorial of the New Milford and Potatuck Indians[22] to the Connecticut authorities, not only gave population numbers of those still residing at the Falls and at Potatuck village (there were still thirty Potatuck remaining at the Great Falls settlement and forty at Potatuck village), but this Memorial also represented a concerted community effort to obtain a teacher and a Congregational minister for the tribe from the Colonial Assembly. Additionally, if this May 1742 Memorial is considered with an April 1742 request for a Moravian missionary, the evidence is present to conclude that rival religious factions were present among the Potatuck, a clear indication of a functioning tribal community. One group was asking for a Moravian missionary, the other a teacher and Congregational minister. Supporting this conclusion was the known hostility by Chere (Cherry), the Potatuck sachem, towards the Moravians as noted by Myron Mack in his June-February 1743 journal.[23]

As early as 1722, there was evidence of religious friction within the tribe, even within the Potatuck sagamore Wereamaug's family. Under the influence of the Reverend Daniel Boardman, minister of First Congregational Church of New Milford, Wereamaug wanted one of his sons to receive an English education. Wereamaug's wife adamantly forbade it. As noted earlier, Wereamaug took ill in 1722. Although he asked for Reverend Boardman's presence (Boardman, Letter of November 4, 1722), in response, his wife bought in the Potatuck tribal shaman *Womsuckaway* to perform a traditional curing ceremony.

The Moravian missionary Myron Mack's journal is a very important primary source document for this period (circa 1743). Besides supporting the presence of rival factions among the Potatuck, Mack showed that there were at this time separate political leaders at both Potatuck and Schaghticoke. In his journal, he referred to "The Capt of Potatick" (Chere, as opposed to "Our Captain in Pachgathgoch...." Mack had to get the permission of the sachem of Potatuck to visit the village, and in turn, he had to obtain

permission of the Captain at Schaghticoke to go there. The evidence
also suggests there was not a close relationship between Potatuck
and Schaghticoke. As a postscript to this journal, the records
indicate that on February 21, 1743, the Moravians were visited by
twenty-one Potatuck Indians as an indicator of their desire to have a
missionary among them.

The Pachgatgoch (Schaghticoke mission) diary for July 4, 1751[24]
noted "....Lea went to Wudbeery...there old Kihur [Kehore] was
extremely friendly...." A similar entry in Bruninger's and Rundt's
diary of July 16, 1755[25] noted "...Old Erdmuthe went to Potatik to
visit her brother...," "Christian [the brother of Chere, the sachem of
Potatuck] and his family went back to Woodberry to join his
company...." Both entries suggest the continued presence of a
Potatuck community within the town of Woodbury.

Finally, Ezra Stiles, the president of Yale University, wrote in
his *Intineraries*[26] (1760) of his 1758 visit to Potatuck, "Cheerow
Sachem at Newtown or pudaduc between Newtown and Woodbury
in 1758." In May of 1759 the last of the Potatuck lands in
Woodbury were conveyed to a town committee.[27] "Cherre," the last
Potatuck sachem, moved to Schaghticoke, there joining his son Sam
Tcherry and brother Petrus Sherman.[28]

The conclusion to be drawn on the basis of the historical
evidence is that the Potatuck continued to exist after the 1705
conveyance of the lands at Weantinock. Moreover the tribe
continued to do so long after the advent of a political community at
Schaghticoke. In 1742 seventy Potatuck remained in two villages
under a recognized political leadership. In 1743 Myron Mack's
journal tells us that not only was there a political leader at Potatuck,
but one at Schaghticoke too. Two communities were under separate
political leadership. The historical record also tells us that Potatuck
village was still there in 1751. We know from the Stiles observation
that the political demise of the Potatuck did not occur until 1758.
The question still remains: Who were the Schaghticoke? They were
certainly not the Potatuck tribe.

N

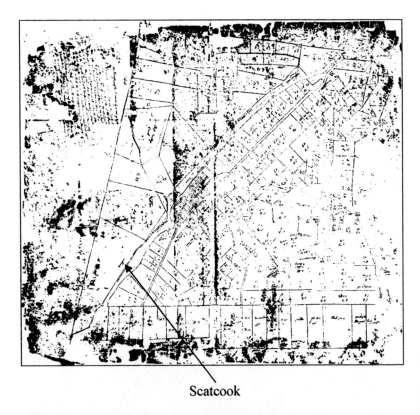

Scatcook

Map 4. Town of Kent, Office of the Town Clerk, Land survey of Kent Connecticut, circa 1752. Schaghticoke reservation ("Scatcook") is in the lower left-hand corner.

Chapter Four

Country Lands

"a parcel of Indians"

As early as 1725, Connecticut's colonial authorities observed:

> ...And whereas we have intelligence from Albany that the enemie are come all out of Canada before the Boston gentlemen got to Canada, and the Skatacuk Indians are drawn off, and there is discovery of Indians in the wilderness above of north of Litchfield and New Milford....[1]

The "Skatacuk" were those of the expatriate Indian village of Schaghticoke in New York. Of importance is the first mention of Indians present in the lands in northwestern Connecticut later to be associated with the Schaghticoke. Who were they?

In May of 1636, the Connecticut General Assembly received the following communication of additional Indian movement into the area:[2]

> "This Assembly being informed that a parcel of Indians that sometime dwelt at New Milford are removed and settled on the west side of Ousatonic River..."

These New Milford Indians were not the first arrivals there.

A contemporary account claims that a "Weantinock" tribe migrated upriver from New Milford and morphed into a Schaghticoke tribe.[3] The Schaghticoke Tribal Nation in their petition for federal recognition steadfastly held to this thesis. Is this true? As this 1736 communication noted, a "parcel"[4] ("a small party") of Indians from New Milford moved up the Housatonic River. Presumably, these new arrivals encountered those Indians who had preceded them in 1725.

The historical record mentions no settled Indian village at this upriver locale prior to 1736. There was a report of Indians of unknown tribal affiliation in the area as early as 1725.[5] This report made no mention of any settled habitation. The lands of Weantinock were conveyed to the proprietors of New Milford in 1705. The two dates, 1705 and 1736 obviously do not square. This parcel of Indians could not have been from the village (or tribe) at Weantinock. It had been sold thirty-one years previous. There could not have been a "Weantinock" tribe. Weantinock was a village of the Potatuck tribe. The historical record clearly supports this. In addition, in 1742 there were still thirty Potatuck remaining at the Great Falls settlement and forty at Potatuck village. Perhaps this migrating parcel was from the village at the Great Falls in New Milford. If so, given that this village as well as the village at Potatuck were still functioning in 1742, the up-river movement of this "parcel" did not represent a tribal migration/morph to Schaghticoke as claimed by the Schaghticoke Tribal Nation in their petition for federal recognition.

Vacume dollicium

The May 1736 General Assembly statement[6] noted that a small group ("parcel") of Potatuck Indians was for the first time moving into and occupying lands on the west side of the Housatonic River. Why was this movement noteworthy for the colony? Why is it so pertinent today? The land where these Indians settled was at that time unoccupied by any established Indian settlement. We can recall that no mention was made of an Indian settlement there in the 1725 Indian census nor was there mention of one in the 1725 Resolve of the Connecticut General Assembly. The 1725 census did note the presence of a village called *Weataug* ten miles upriver from this location. The line of travel to get to Weataug would have had to pass by the bend in the river where the village at Schaghticoke was later established. In his historical writings, Benjamin Trumbull indicated that no settlement was there when he asked the question:

> What became of the Indians, who were first on the ground before the English had any settlement [at Kent] there, is not known. When they moved away or to what place, cannot be ascertained...[7]

Given this state of affairs, the Colony of Connecticut considered these lands, excluding two earlier land grants, to be *vacume dollicium*, that is, empty and uninhabited country lands. Trumbull's question quoted above supports this position. So did the General Assembly's note of the Indian settlement. Subsequently there was no need for the colony to obtain any deed of conveyance for the local lands on the west side of the Housatonic from the region's Indians in that area. Those remnant Indians moving up into the area in 1736 were also newcomers to the area. As a matter of historical fact, we do not know the identities of those "New Milford" Indians, their numbers or leadership. For all we know they could have been an Indian family looking for better agricultural or hunting lands.

The Colony of Connecticut regarded most of the lands in this area as being *country lands*, that is, lands that were owned by the colony but were not yet granted out. There were two exceptions. Two colonial land grants were made prior to the 1736 New Milford Indian settlement in this area. The first was the 1673 grant to the heirs of Stephen Hart of Farmington[8] and a 1734 grant to Elisha Williams.[9] Both grants were for lands on the west side of the Housatonic River facing the location of the future town of Kent. The Williams grant encompassed much of the alluvial bottomlands of the present-day site of Kent School and are the subject of present-day land claims brought by the Schaghticoke Tribal Nation. Williams's grant occurred two years before the Indians from New Milford settled there. The adjacent Hart grant abutted the Williams grant on its northern boundary.

That the colony allowed these Indians to remain was due to the nature of the land ownership. These lands were presently non-granted and vacant of colonial settlement. The colony also warned settlers not to settle or purchase from the Indians any land in the area.[10] Why? These were colony-owned lands. Settlers could not establish a homestead on them unless they received a land grant from the colony. Additionally, Connecticut law forbade individuals from making land purchases directly from any Indians unless they were doing so for the benefit of a town or for the colonial authorities.[11] The colony's intent was not to establish a reservation for these Indians. To do so, a land survey must be undertaken to demarcate its boundaries and the Connecticut General Assembly itself would have had to pass a resolve or an act to that effect. This was not done until 1752. Yet, the Schaghticoke Tribal Nation claimed that by allowing this "parcel of Indians" to reside upon these lands, the Colony of Connecticut created a reservation for a Schaghticoke tribe. The Schaghticoke Tribal Nation used this "parcel" incident to claim that the Schaghticoke were merely a continuation or successors in interest of the Potatuck/Weantinock tribe. By doing so, they claim that they are an historic tribe predating the advent of colonial era contact. This research shows this was not the case in fact. If what the Schaghticoke Tribal Nation says is true, why would the Schaghticoke have felt the need to petition the Connecticut General Assembly in 1752 for such lands? Additionally, by allowing this "parcel" to reside on these country lands in 1736, the Schaghticoke claimed, the Colony *de facto* recognized them as an Indian tribe. That, they claimed, amounted to state recognition. The Interior Board of Indian Appeals in its decision vacating Bureau of Indian Affairs's initial recognition determination soundly rejected this notion.

"the pleasure of this Assembly"

In 1752, the Colony of Connecticut needed some of these country lands at Schaghticoke for granting. The Connecticut General Assembly also received a petition from the Moravian missionaries and their Indian convert community[12] who were living "on ye Countrey Lands on ye west Side of ousatunack River at a place called Scaticook..." for a grant of land. In response to this request the colony rejected the grant request; instead it established a reservation for them within defined surveyed boundaries on colony-owned lands but only "during the pleasure of this Assembly...."[13] In other words, the Moravians and their Indian converts were allowed as *tenants at will* to reside upon these reserved lands. The Connecticut General Assembly reserved the right to either disestablish or alter the size of the reservation at will. It must be remembered that the colony/state was, and still is the title holder to these lands. Most importantly, 1752, not 1736 marked the beginning of a recognized Schaghticoke reservation at Kent. Current land claims bought by the Schaghticoke Tribal Nation to reclaim lands purportedly taken from them lack a basis of historical validity.

Thus colonial claims to the area preceded the first recorded 1636 migration of "Indians that sometime dwelt at New Milford" into the area. The early Moravian missionaries from Shecomeko (1743) mentioned only the presence of a seasonal "winter village" in the area.[14] There was no tribal movement upriver from New Milford. An Indian reservation was not established in the area until 1752. The reservation was established at the request of the Moravian missionaries for the use by their Christian converts.

From the Indians' perspective, whose tribal lands were those upon which this "parcel" of "New Milford" Indians settled in 1636?

Mahican Turf

We have seen that the Colony of Connecticut considered the lands on the west side of the Housatonic River to be vacant and unsettled. These lands were part of Connecticut Colony. Yet from the Indians' perspective, which Indian tribe considered these lands to be part of their traditional tribal territory? Were they Potatuck or Mahican?

The historical record depicts a boundary interaction between the Mahican and Potatuck tribes in this northwestern Connecticut region. Where was it? A Mahican-Potatuck boundary nexus appears to have begun on the east side of the Housatonic River just south of the Mahican village of *Weataug*. This village was located on the west side of the Houstonic near the present-day boundary of the towns of Sharon and Salisbury, Connecticut. It was cited in the 1725 Indian census. Phillip Colee in his 1977 Ph.D dissertation[15] also noted the presence of such a tribal boundary:

> Downstream from the upper Housatonic settlement, in northwestern Connecticut, the situation was in flux throughout the 1730's. In the latter part of the decade a number of parcels of land in the vicinity of the new settlements on or near the Housatonic River were sold to the Connecticut colonists by the Indians of the area. There are weak indications of the existence of a political boundary

between the Indians in the vicinity of the upper Housatonic settlement and those near the new Connecticut settlements.

The June 19, 1716 Benjamin Fairweather purchase[16] gives a clear indication that such was the case. This conveyance extended thirty miles north from the north boundary of New Milford. Its west boundary was the Houstonic River. The width of the purchase was three miles. There were two Indian leaders who served as both attestors and subscribers to this act of conveyance. The first was *Wereamaug*, the sagamore of the Potatuck tribe. Second, was a kinsman of his, *Nepotoe*, a Mahican from the village of *Weataug*. Nepatoe's participation in roles of both attestor and subscriber to the conveyance indicates that a portion of the land involved included lands considered to belong to the Mahican tribe.

Proof of Nepatoe being a Mahican is demonstrated by three documents: the October 22, 1720 conveyance[17] to Hartford and Windsor; the August 29, 1720[18] Rowlee Ducher purchase; and the January 27, 1721[19] Mahican conveyance.

Briefly, the October 1720 document has both "Werreamaug" and "Nepatoe" attesting and subscribing to a land conveyance. In this document, they both reserved lands within the purcehase area. Nepatoe reserved a tract just to the south of lands belonging to "...Rowlee Dutcher's...." on the east side of the Housatonic River. Rowlee Ducher's August 1720 purchase confirmed the location. The January 1721 document depicted Nepatoe (*"Nequatoo"*) as one of seventeen Mahican subscribers to the conveyance of lands on the west side of the Houstonic River south of Weataug village. The tract of land conveyed ran south along the river for three miles. Most importantly, this deed of conveyance was attested to by *Metoxon,* the sagamore of the Mahican tribe.

That Mahican tribal territory encompassed the present-day towns of Salisbury and Sharon, Connecticut is not questionable. Sharon, which borders north of present-day town of Kent (the site of Schaghticoke), was conveyed to the proprietors there by Metoxon, the tribe's sagamore.[20] On October 8, 1743, Isaac Vernerun purchased two thousand acres on the west side of the Housatonic in Kent from Stephen, a Mahican sachem from the village of Squapamack in the nearby Province of New York.[21] It was not a valid deed, but it is historically important. Stephen, whose brother was the sachem of the Mahican village of Wequanach (in present-day Sharon), also conveyed lands in the south of Sharon along the Sharon/Kent boundary line. Stephen was also known as *Wasampa*. He was a Moravian convert who was baptized at the Shekomeko mission as Joshua.[22] Stephen/Wasampa/Joseph was also known as *Nahun*. He was married to a Moravian Wompanach woman by the name of Salome at Shekomeko. By 1749, both had removed to Bethlehem, Pennsylvania. In the May 15, 1745 Fuller and Lasell petition,[23] Stephen was depicted as "...Sachem of ye Tribe of Indians called Scattacooks & was the Indian owner of sd Land..." Under Wasampa's authority at Schaghticoke, as Martin Mack, a Moravian minister, noted "...in all, there live about 200 savages here."[24] These documents leave no doubt that the lands on the west bank of the Houstonic River in Kent, including lands being utilized by an Indian community numbering 200 at Schaghticoke were, circa 1745, part of Mahican tribal territory.

Bordering south on Kent are the present-day towns of Sherman and New Fairfield. Originally, they were one township (New Fairfield). On April 24, 1729,[25] the remaining non-conveyed lands within the original grant were conveyed by "Cockkenenon and Mauwwehue oners and proper proiators of all the unsold lands...." Cockkenenon was the principal signatory.

The attestors to this act of conveyance, Cockenon and Mauwwehue, present an interesting situation. Cockenon was a Mahican Indian from the village of Shecomeko. He was an attestor to the fact in the petition of *Shawas* (Abraham) dated October 17, 1743[26] ("*Kockanonh*"). This petition and Cockenon's attestment dealt with his expert knowledge of the village boundaries and the history of Mahican land conveyances to the notorious land speculators, the "Little Nine Partnership" in New York. Mauwwehue (Mauwee) was also an attestor to the same fact, in the same petition, and for the same reason. He attested to his statement under his Mahican name "*Ammauasemon*."[27] Loskiel states that Mauwee's parents were of the Mahican village of Shecomeko. (Mauwee, aka Gideon, will be dealt with in greater detail in the next chapter.) The other three attestors to this petition were identifiable Mahican. On the April 1729 New Fairfield document,[28] there were eight witnesses to this act of conveyance. Of the eight, one was an identifiable Mahican (*Catorukese*), and two were expatriate Pequannock Indians (*Shonin* and *Siecuss*). The remaining five are unidentifiable. Most importantly their names never appeared on any Potatuck, Paugussett, or Pequannock-related document. On this basis the document appears to be Mahican and indicative of New Fairfield being within the bounds Mahican tribal territory.

It is clear by the preceding that the Mahican tribe controlled a significant portion of Northwestern Connecticut, including the lands that were to become the Schaghticoke reservation. Conversely, the Potatuck tribe had its own defined tribal boundary. When lands were conveyed to Connecticut Colony or the towns, both tribes respected these boundaries and worked together to protect their interests.

On another level, this research places the claims made by the Schaghticoke Tribal Nation in a quandary. If, as the Schaghticoke Tribal Nation claims, they were a historic tribe, then on the basis of their residing on lands belonging to the Mahican tribe, they were part of the Mahican tribe under the political authority of not only Stephen the local Mahican sachem, but also of Metoxon, the Mahican sagamore. On this basis they would have failed on the political autonomy requirement as set forth in the federal recognition requirement 25 CFR 83.7 (c).

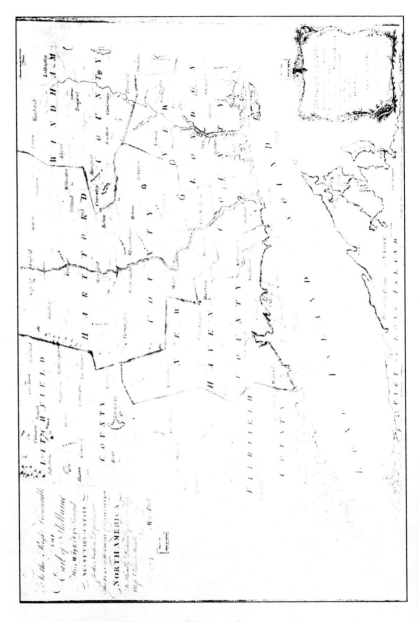

Map 5. 1766 Royal Survey of Connecticut.
Library of Congress, Map Division.

Chapter Five

Brother Gideon's Calling

The Advent of the Moravians

In working towards an understanding of the formation of the Indian community at Schaghticoke, we have looked at historical setting, displacement, and territory. We will now add a catalyst to this list. That catalyst was the Moravian Church, a missionary sect whose origins go back to medieval Europe and the ancient region called Monrovia. They spoke German for the most part, an ancient form of the language, that even contemporary German speakers have difficulty understanding. This church founded Bethlehem, Pennsylvania. Its North American headquarters remains there to this day. The genius of the Moravian missionary activities among Indian tribes was their manner of gaining converts. Unlike other denominations, they lived in a like manner among their converts. The conversion they sought was internal. The Moravians were the leaders of their mission communities, no doubt, but they ran the mission communities through Indian converts (stewards). As the converts internalized the Moravian teachings, they changed outwardly in behavior. Other churches put the cart before the donkey, forcing converts to change outwardly before they could internalize their new religious and cultural ideology. The Moravians' approach was to ease the converts into a new ideological setting, thereby reducing the psychological trauma of such acculturative transformations.

In 1740, Moravian missionaries from Pennsylvania established a major mission site at the Mahican village of *Shecomeko*. This village was located near present-day Dover Plains, New York. At the time of the Moravians' first visit (1740) to this Mahican village, there was an Indian population numbering under 100. This population included eastern (Wompanach) and upland (Hooglander) Indians[1] as well as Mahican. Prior to the Moravian activities at Shecomeko, this village served as a gathering place, receiving and absorbing refugee Indians from the surrounding region. It functioned in the same manner as Schaghticoke (New York) and Stockbridge in Massachusetts. A trail from this village ran eastward to the Housatonic River, terminating at the future site of Schaghticoke in Connecticut.

Shecomeko was a typical contact-era Mahican village. Prior to the advent of the fur trade, Mahican villages were large multi-clan (Turtle/Wolf/Bear) matrilineal, matrilocal-based independent settlements.[2] Lineage families resided in longhouse residence clusters. As a result of sustained contact (c.1700), political authority became centralized under a central leader. Matrilocal residence patterns gave way to neo-local single-family wigwams.[3] Political authority and leadership was still reckoned from matrilineal affiliation.

In 1743, a smaller mission was established among the Potatuck. It was of short (one year) duration due to local religious opposition to the Moravians' presence by the neighboring Congregational colonists. This smaller mission at New Milford acted to funnel some Potatuck individuals and families to Shecomeko. There were eight identifiable Potatuck at the Shecomeko mission in 1743.[4] Seven of these individuals were later listed on the 1751 *Pachgatgoch* (Schaghticoke) Connecticut Mission register.[5] (See Appendix B.) By 1748, there were at Shekomeko forty-one "Mahik," thirty-three "Wompanach," ten "Sopus," twelve "Delaware," one "Mennissing," (Minisink) and two "Hooglanders" listed as Indian members of the Shekomeko mission.[6] Many of these Wompanach had taken Mahican spouses and had become integrated into Mahican matrilineages.[7]

A second Moravian mission was established at the Mahican village of *Wequanach* (also known *Sichem* or *Gnadensee)* on the east shore of Indian Pond in Sharon, Connecticut. The land encompassing this mission site as well as most of the town of Sharon was part of Mahican tribal territory. On October 26, 1738, a conveyance of the lands in Sharon was made. This conveyance was acknowledged by *Metankson* (Metoxon), the Mahican tribal sagamore.[8] He was assisted in this task by the presence of another Indian named *Umpachenee,* a leading Mahican sachem responsible for the polyglot Indian village at Schaghticoke, New York and later

Stockbridge, Massachusetts. Metoxon's role as a Mahican sagamore was confirmed by Thomas Fitch[9] in 1742 when he observed:

> ...would humbly report to your Honrs that we find that one Metoxson alias Collonel alias Corlow is allowed by all to be ye chiefe Sachem of the Indians in those parts and that he and his tribe or Nation are the claimers of those lands not sold....

A second conveyance for a remaining one-mile strip on the south border of Sharon adjoining the northern boundary of Kent was obtained in February of 1739 for " ...ye Govr & Company...." This deed was acknowledged by the local Mahican sachem of Wequanach, *Nauness* (aka Naural, John, Johannes) and his brother *Waapcham Stephenus* (aka Stephen or Stephen John), sachem of the lands in the Schaghticoke region.[10]

John Sergent,[11] the missionary at Stockbridge, reported that as early as 1739 his mission received regular visits from Indians residing at *Wequatenauk* in northwestern Connecticut. By 1742, Sergent noted that substantial numbers of Indians (twenty-seven) from Wequatenauk (Wequanach) had taken up residence at his mission. In 1749 there were at least fifteen Potatuck residing among a larger mixed Mahican (Christian and non-Christian) population at Wequanach (Sharon) mission. By comparison, during the same year there were only eight Potatuck/Wompanach residing at Schaghticoke. The Moravian Pachgatgoch (Schaghticoke) mission was not established until 1750.[12] (See Appendix D.) Of the fifteen Potatuck in residence at Wequanach in 1749, thirteen were later listed in residence at Schaghticoke on the 1751 Moravian mission register. The principal reason for the increase in the 1751 population at Schaghticoke was the influx of Indian converts from the Wequanach mission when it was disestablished in 1751, one year prior to the colony's 1752 establishment of the reservation at Schaghticoke.

Although the majority of the mixed non-Christian Mahican/Potatuck population living at Wequanach was reported to have joined the Oneida Iroquois, others migrated to the Moravian mission community of *Gnadenhutten* in Pennsylvania.[13] Some of the remaining Mahican converts at the Wequanach mission joined their Mahican brethren at the Shecomeko mission while others removed to Stockbridge. In 1751, at Gideon's (Mauwee) calling, other Indians, including thirteen Potatuck converts, joined their Christian brethren at the Pachgatgoch (Schaghticoke) mission. Gideon Mauwee was now the Moravians' appointed steward of the Indian convert community.[14] A distinct functioning Indian missionary community at Schaghticoke began to emerge.

The Question of Mauwee

The name, Mauwee, is synonymous with the founding of the Schaghticoke mission community. His name invokes controversy. Mystery and debate surrounds his background and the role he played in the Schaghticoke community's development. Who was he? What was his tribal affiliation? We do know that ultimately he became the "captain" or "steward" of the Indians of the Moravian mission community at Schaghticoke. But there our certainty about him has always ended.

The Dutch anthropologist, Franz Wojciechowski, claims that Mauwee was a member of his purported "Weantinock" tribe.[15] He further claims that Mauwee succeeded his Weantinock tribal leader Wereamaug (who was actually the sagamore of the Potatuck tribe) as tribal leader of this purported tribe after his death in 1725 (he actually died in 1722). Wojciechowski claims that the Potatuck and Weantinock were two separate historical tribes. Wojciechowski also claims that Mauwee and his Weantinock tribe migrated upriver to Schaghticoke, settling there in 1736.[16] He concludes that the Schaghticoke evolved out of his "Weantinock" tribe. Other relevant records suggests otherwise.

When the Moravians (Myron Mack) visited the village at Schaghticoke in 1743, they encountered a man named Mauwee ("old captan Mawessman") and also some members of his immediate family. Mauwee appears to of been the patriarch of an extended family of eight residing at Schaghticoke. Among those present were his wife Lazara, his son Joshua (Job) and daughter Maria, as well as three expatriate Potatuck. They were baptized into the Moravian Church by Mack during his visit.[17] Mauwee was reported by Moravian sources[18] to be the son of Isaac (*Siem, Apawanamen*) of Shecomeko and a Mahican mother named

Rebecca.[19] Mauwee never appeared on any Potatuck-related document prior to the 1705 conveyance and demise of Weantinock village. Until the May 1742 Memorial to the Connecticut General Assembly, his name never appeared in direct association with any Potatuck Indian settlements.

Mauwee's early historical appearances seemed to have been linked with Mahican tribal activities rather than those of the Potatuck tribe. Five documents support this conclusion:

June 19, 1716 - Fairweather Purchase
October 22, 1720 - Hartford/Windsor Conveyance
June 23, 1722 - Wereamaug Quit-claim
April 24, 1729 - New Fairfield Conveyance
October 17, 1743 - Shecomeko Petition of Shawas

Prior to the 1716 purchase,[20] Mauwee never appeared on any documents related to either Potatuck or Weantinock villages. Mauwee appeared as a witness to the act of the 1716 Fairweather conveyance. The attestors to the act were Wereamaug, sagamore of the Potatuck tribe, and Nepatoe. We have noted beforehand that Nepatoe was a Mahican and was associated with the Mahican village of *Weataug*. The presence of both Wereamaug and Nepatoe on this conveyance meant that lands belonging to both tribes were affected by this conveyance.

At the October 22, 1720 Hartford/Windsor conveyance,[21] Wereamaug and Nepatoe were again present, as was Mauwee. Again, as explicitly stated in the conveyance and by the presence of subscribers representing both tribes' lands, Indians belonging to each tribe were involved.

Significantly, the June 23, 1722 quit-claim[22] by Wereamaug of a portion of the lands he reserved in the October 22, 1720 conveyance[23] did not contain either Nepatoe's or Mauwee's names. Only Chere, the Potatuck—Wereamaug's son and future tribal leader—along with five other Potatuck were present, even though the quit-claim included a portion of the lands involved in the 1720 conveyance that was attended to by both Wereamaug and Nepatoe (and Mauwee). The lands in this 1722 quit-claim were in Potatuck territory.

Up to this point, the pattern of Mauwee's presence or non-presence suggests he was linked to Nepatoe. In addition, the location of the lands conveyed upon which Mauwee's name appeared seemed to be localized to the peripheries of Potatuck tribal territory.

The April 24, 1729 New Fairfield Conveyance[24] supports this pattern. Despite Wojciechowski's claims, this conveyance was not a "Weantinock," or Potatuck for that matter, deed. There were two subscribers to the deed: *Cockkenon*, who beforehand was shown to be a Mahican of Shecomeko, and *Mauwee* (*Mauwehue*). Of the five witnesses to the act, one, *Catorukese* has also been shown to be a Mahican. Two of the other witness's were expatriate Pequannock Indians and the five others tribal affiliations remain unknown. Their names do not appear on any Mahican or Potatuck documents.

It was discussed earlier that both Mauwee and Cockkenon were attestors to the fact on a 1743 Mahican petition concerning Shecomeko. In such an action, they, along with the other Mahican attestors, were considered knowledgeable individuals of Shecomeko's affairs. Why would one "Weantinock" Indian, Mauwee, among all the other attestors who were Mahican, be considered to have "expert" knowledge of a Mahican village's (Shecomeko) land conveyances and boundaries? Answer: Mauwee was a Mahican.

This leads us back to Loskiel's assertion that Mauwee was the son of Isaac of Shecomeko. He was married to a Mahican woman, Rebecca, also from Shecomeko.[25] Following the matrilineal rules of the Mahican tribe, Mauwee would, as the son of Rebecca, have belonged to her Mahican matrilineage at Shecomeko.

Looking collectively at these documents we find Mauwee's early appearances linked to Nepatoe, a Mahican of Weataug, a Mahican village (1716, 1720). From a geographical standpoint, Mauwee's appearances were on the edges of Mahican/Potatuck tribal territories; furthermore, he attests a deed with identifiable Mahicans in New Fairfield (1729). A respected Moravian historian (Loskiel) places him within Mahican territory and identifies his father (Isaac of Shecomeko). Documents within the Moravian archives not only identify the wife (Rebecca of Shecomeko) of his purported father, but also have him (Mauwee) interacting as a knowledgeable person with identifiable Mahicans on a petition (1743 Shecomeko) involving land issues of a Mahican village, Shecomeko, the residence of his father (and mother).

In July of 1741, Mauwee and three of the unidentified witnesses from the 1729 New Fairfield Conveyance identified themselves in this conveyance as "Indians all of Scaticook." This was the first known association of Mauwee with Schaghticoke. In this document, he did not at this time claim or imply any position of leadership among this group. Oddly, the following year his name appeared on the May 13, 1742 Petition of the Indians at New Milford and Potatuck, a tribe that was, according to Wojciechowski, supposed to have migrated to Schaghticoke in 1736. Yet, the following year, in 1743, Mauwee was at Schaghticoke, but not as a leader.

"Umpachenee's cousin"

In October of 1743 Stephen, the Mahican sachem, was considered to be in the words of the Fuller and Lasell petition[26] (May 1745) "Sachem of ye tribe of Indians called Scattacooks & was the Indian owner of sd land...." In addition and of significant importance, Fraizer[27] noted: "and several miles near Kent was a village of more than a hundred eastern Indians who became known as Scaticooks, whose chief was Umpachenee's cousin...." Umpachenee was a Mahican sachem. At this point in time he was the sachem over the polyglot Indian community located at Schaghticoke, New York. Fraizer's comment can be interpreted two ways. For the sake of argument, if Fraizer was referring to Stephen, it would support the position of Mahican control over Schaghticoke. On the other hand, if Fraizer was addressing Mauwee as a leader there, it would confirm via his relation to Umpachenee that Mauwee was a Mahican. The Moravian records confirm that Mauwee was residing there in 1743.[28] If this is true and Mauwee's father was, as Loskiel stated, Isaac of Shecomeko with his Mahican wife Rebecca, then according to the rules of matrilineal descent among the Mahican, Umpachenee[29] was the son of Mauwee's mother's sister. His father's lineage or tribal affiliation would have had no bearing on this relationship. Descent and affiliation were reckoned via the maternal descent line. Schaghticoke was a Mahican village. Also of

note was Fraizer's assessment that the village was inhabited by
"eastern Indians." Another question is raised: Who were the one
hundred Indians residing at Schaghticoke, circa 1743? One year
earlier the entire Potatuck tribe residing at the Great Falls and
Potatuck consisted of only a total of seventy Indians.[30] Three years
later Martin Mack, a Moravian minister, noted of Schaghticoke
"...in all, there live about 200 savages here."[31] This observation
indicated a vast increase in population within a few short years.
They were certainly not Potatuck.

"Sachum of Saticook"

The October 1743 document depicting Stephen as the sachem at
Schaghticoke makes it clear that Mauwee (Gideon) was not a leader
there circa 1743. We know that Mauwee was also residing there in
1743. He may have been the captain of the convert Moravian
Indians at Schaghticoke referred to in Mack's journal, but not of the
entire Indian community. That is seven years after the first reported
settling of Indians from New Milford in the area (1736). Stephen
was the recognized Mahican sachem at Schaghticoke. He was
clearly associated with the Mahican tribal sagamore, Metoxon. His
brother was the sachem of Wequanach in Sharon. This suggests that
this parcel of Indians from New Milford were not the first Indians to
settle on the west side of the Housatonic River opposite Kent.

In 1746, Stephen removed to Bethlehem, Pennsylvania, where he
became a Moravian convert.[32] Did Stephen's departure leave a
political leadership void in the region, which Mauwee as a Mahican
unsuccessfully attempted to exploit? On February 16, 1749 (Samuel
Alger Purchase), Mauwee claimed for the first time to be the
"Sachum of Saticook." The question here is: Over *whom* was
Mauwee claiming to be "sachum"?

Mauwee's purported rise to leadership at Schaghticoke was not
as Wojciechowski claimed[33] by the mere continuation of the
"Weantinock" tribal leadership role he purportedly assumed after
Wereamaug's death. Wojciechowski's assertion that Schaghticoke
represented a political continuation of a "Weantinock tribe" is
unsupportable and unfounded. The persona of that purported
leadership, Mauwee, was not of that village. Weantinock was sold

in 1705. There is no evidence that placed Mauwee among the original 1636 migrants to Schaghticoke. The data strongly suggests that he was of the Mahican tribe and may have ascended to that role due to a breakdown of Mahican tribal leadership in the region. This, as we shall see, was not the case.

Two questions beg an answer. First, if Stephen was the sachem at Schaghticoke prior to 1743, over whom was he sachem until his departure in 1746? Second, who were the 100 Indians residing at Schaghticoke, among whom it was presumed that Mauwee and his six-member extended family were residing? Or were they? By 1746, the year of Stephen's departure for Bethlehem, that number of Indians at Schaghticoke had risen to 200. Who were these Indians? The following two chapters will address these questions.

Demographically, we see that it was impossible for the Schaghticoke Tribal Nation to claim that the historic Schaghticoke were but a continuation of the Potatuck. The number of residents at Schaghticoke far exceeded any numbers ever recorded for the Potatuck. Yet, as we have seen, the Potatuck as a tribe were still in existence at two village locales. At the same time, another claim was made that Mauwee was a Potatuck or Weantinock Indian who succeeded Wereamaug as tribal sagamore or sachem. The evidence is quite substantial that Mauwee belonged to the Mahican tribe.

Chapter Six

A "Bow" in the River

"our blessed Gideon" and "this little flock of Indians"

According to the Moravian documents, in 1743 the initial convert population at Schaghticoke was a small expatriate family of eight led by their family patriarch (Mauwee): "this little flock of Indians," as Martin Mack observed. These eight people constituted the founding core of the Moravian Indian mission at Schaghticoke. By 1750, their numbers had grown to thirteen. One year later in 1751, the year of the closing of the Wequanach mission, the number in residence in the convert community had swelled to forty-nine. What were the enabling factors that assisted this community's development?

One principal factor was, as a result of sustained colonial contact, the gradual breakdown of traditional Potatuck and Mahican political and social institutions and the behavioral constraints they sanctioned. This situation allowed for the fissioning off of individuals and families from the traditional lineage structure. This was readily apparent for the Potatuck after the 1705 sale of Weantinock. The 1722 death of the tribe's last sagamore, Wereamaug, may have created a tribal leadership void, that although filled by his son Chere, nonetheless weakened tribal social and behavioral constraints that enabled individuals to act independently. This state of affairs facilitated the dispersal of segments of the tribe to other tribes, especially Mahican tribal villages. These villages in turn were themselves experiencing growing cultural tensions and colonial acculturative pressures. Kinship ties developed as a result of residence and intermarriage with Mahican lineages at Shecomeko, Wequanach, and also with the Taconic. The populations of Mahican villages themselves were, as early as 1700,[1] starting to fission due to growing land conveyances, drunkenness, and famine. Many moved to the Oneida Iroquois country, others joined the St. Francis Abenaki in Canada. The advent of the Moravian missions in western New York and northwestern Connecticut provided an additional alternate route to adapting to a changing socio-cultural environment. Into this growing cultural schism came the Moravian missionaries.

The Moravians were a major force for accommodation to a rapidly disintegrating cultural environment. Essentially, as tribes came into sustained contact with European culture they either dispersed or disintegrated. The Moravian missionaries provided their converts with an ideology that produced a new identity and new social and symbolic norms to guide their lives (i.e. stability) that helped these remnant Indians adapt to the dynamics of socio-cultural change. This process of assimilation to a Christian-based value system was similar to that practiced by the Iroquois tribes in regards to war captives and refugees they adopted and assimilated into their clan/lineage system.[2] The adoptive individual was given a new identity, ritually reborn (identical in form to the Moravian rite of Baptism of converts) into a clan-based kinship system. The old identity was considered dead, i.e. purged, hence the bestowal of a new name, usually of a deceased member of the lineage. Backsliding was a serious offense. The Moravians used mostly Old Testament names in bestowing new identities. Their records clearly convey this notion. One record in particular bears out this practice.[3] This document recorded the baptism and conversion of Mauwee and the others of his family at Schaghticoke in 1743. The list was divided into two columns. The first was titled: "names were" the second "and are now." Thus *Marveseman* (Mauwee) became Gideon.[4] He had made the transition from savage to brother. In Martin Mack's 1743 journal of these proceedings, he stated:

> we were lodg'd by Capt Mawessman. He, she & 2 Children are no longer recon'd Dead People.[5]

For expounding his newfound beliefs, Mauwee was harassed by members of the non-convert Indian community who were also residing at Schaghticoke. In one case, an Indian put a gun to his head and threatened to blow it off if he continued to speak of Jesus.[6]

Mauwee himself recognized his new identity in relation to his past. In a 1757 letter to Bethlehem, Pennsylvania, he wrote of this distinction:

...We should be very glad to hear that all our friends and Acquaintenses were all in Bethlehem and not amongst the other wild Indians.[7]

From the time of Mauwee's 1743 Moravian baptism until his death in 1760, the historical record strongly suggests that Mauwee was not the leader of all the Indians residing at Schaghticoke, but only a steward (captain) to those of the Moravian Indian community residing there. His prominence in this particular community was due to his selection as a community steward by the Moravian missionaries:

...our blessed Gideon, and his office as stewart.[8]

In his journal, Martin Mack made the following comment in regards to an extended conversation he had in 1743 with the "Capt of Potatick" (village) who in the past had exhibited hostility towards the missionaries. Mack observed:

Our Captain in Pachgathgoch [referring to Mauwee] wondered very much that he had spoke so much with us...[9]

This comment clearly refers to Mauwee as the leader ("Captain"), "Our" leader of the convert community at the Pachgathgoch mission. The fact that Mauwee was harassed by members of the non-converted Schaghticoke Indian community is indicative of his liminal status to this group and also of his limited political status as the leader only of the minority Moravian Indian community present at Schaghticoke village. In 1743 there were besides the Indian converts, 200 Indians at Schaghticoke. The limited nature of Mauwee's authority at Schaghticoke was aptly demonstrated in a 1752 Moravian petition to the Connecticut General Assembly:

That Capt Mawehu Indian may be appointed, let & declared as Captain for the Indians in Scatticok—whom the others shall obey when he orders any Thing for the Good & Beft of the Race & its inhabitants...[10]

The General Assembly's response was quite interesting. Written at the bottom of the petition copy was the following, "Who is this Captain? Gideon?"

If Mauwee was the "Sachum of Saticook" why would such a petition have been made? The petition clearly delineates his limited authority. What is especially noteworthy was the necessity of asking the General Assembly to give him authority in the colony's name in order to demand obedience to his "orders?"

In 1751 the total Moravian Indian community totaled forty-seven adults and approximately forty children.[11] A 1752 Moravian petition to the General Assembly notes that their community consists of eighteen families.[12] Ezra Stiles recorded a 1754 total Indian population at Schaghticoke of 600, of whom 161 were men.[13] As a gross figure, subtracting the eighty-seven Moravian converts led by Mauwee, this leaves a non-Christian Indian community of approximately 513. The Moravian Indian community was clearly a distinct liminal minority population at Schaghticoke. Mauwee's influence was limited to this Moravian community. There was no Schaghticoke "tribe," only two dissimilar communities.

"Without a teacher to guide them"

This minuscule community of converts became its own self-contained, self-identifying community within a larger, seemingly disorganized community of non-Christianized Indians. These converts constructed their own separate dwellings at what was termed "lower Schagticoke."[14] According to Mack, their stated desire was that "...they wish also to have order & make Shekomeko always their model."[15] A constant concern of the missionaries was to prevent backsliding by their proselytes. When it did occur, the missionaries conversed with the individual; they did not condemn. The Indian converts themselves were equally concerned as Gideon Mauwee lamented, "...that they are now baptized and know about the saviour, but don't know how to continue without a teacher to guide them towards the proper path..."[16] The Moravians preached love rather than damnation. They lived with and among their converts in a like manner. The Moravians strived to learn and preach to their converts in their native tongue. They held twice-daily prayer meetings ("quarter-hours") morning and evening, and periodic "love feasts."[17] They educated the children of their converts.[18] Some could speak both German and English. They preached self-sufficiency. The community (including males who were not normally involved in agriculture) grew and harvested their own corn,[19] co-operatively enclosed their fields with fences,[20] established an apple orchard and harvested blueberries for marketing,[21] gathered their own firewood as a group, collectively hunted and built summerhouses and winter-houses[22] and maintained their own community-based economic activities such as canoe building, basket and broom manufacturing the produce of which they marketed to the local towns (Kent and New Milford).[23] The Moravian converts even buried their own deceased adults and children apart form the main Indian population: "The child's grandfather had to carry the child himself to the grave because no baptized Indian brothers were at home."[24] Only brethren buried brethren. Perhaps this is the most telling statement describing the extent by which the two communities were socially and culturally divided. The Moravian Indian community maintained its own cemetery, which was referred to as "God's Acre."[25] Again, this attests to the degree of separateness between the two communities.

What they (both missionary and convert) created was an exclusive, bonded, family-based community that recognized and permitted certain outward Indian cultural norms; this was especially so for family-based economic activities, rather than the typical non-Indian Moravian practice of a sex-based division of labor, while at the same time inwardly creating a new person. The Moravian missionaries allowed an Indian to remain outwardly so while effecting change upon the individual's inner beliefs. As the conversion process progressed, the convert began to express outwardly these new inner beliefs. These practices produced a social, political and culturally integrated self-identifying Indian community distinctly apart from any other.

The Moravians constantly sought new Indian brothers and sisters for the community but they did not force the issue:

> We were today uncommonly embarrassed by our poor Indians. We begged and implored them to please come to our Savior to be helped by him, but it seems that they don't intend to yet to become people of a blessed heart.[26]

The apparent success of the Moravians' efforts at Schaghticoke had far-reaching consequences for other missionary activities. In 1746, Samuel Hopkins, who succeeded John Sergent as leader of the Stockbridge Indian mission, was none too kind in his comments regarding his downriver competition:

> It is probable we should have had more of them before now, if There had not come some Moravian preachers among some of them near to us. I do not pretend too so much acquaintance with that sort of people as to pass any positive judgment about them; the converts they have made are, I think enthusiastick and bigoted.... They drew off a number of Indians from these parts, and some from this place to Pennsylvania.[27]

As the Schaghticoke mission population grew[28] to forty-seven adults by 1751, the concern for more land[29] for this community came to the forefront, fostering a historically pivotal event in the emergence of the Schaghticoke.

"Where all can speak"

Included in the narrative of a 1752 Moravian community meeting[30] "where all can speak his or her mind,"[31] among these Moravian converts and their missionaries are comments that link the Moravian community to the 1752 petition to the Connecticut General Assembly. This petition led to the setting aside of lands by the Connecticut General Assembly for the use of the Moravian mission community at Schaghticoke. These lands became the Schaghticoke reservation. This narrative clearly stated that:

> ...because they couldn't keep themselves because of their large families on the land, they asked whether they [Moravian Brethren] had a good friend who would go to court for them, who could assist them? Brother Joseph said he had heard that the "Country" had assumed all land in this neighborhood and that they took away again land from those people who had bought it from Br. Gideon without repaying them because they thought it was theirs...Brother Joseph finally suggested

he would get a lawyer for them in New York who could write
a flawless legal petition for them.

This meeting resulted in the May 1752 petition to the General
Assembly.[32] All the Indian petitioners cited on this "Memorial"
were Moravian converts belonging to the Schaghticoke mission.
There were no signatories from the general Indian population. The
signatories represented the mission's eighteen families. The
signatories were as follows:

> Gideon, Josua, Samuel, Martin, Simon, Jeremias, Petrus,
> Gottlob, Christian, Lucas, Gottlieb, Isaaous, Tsherry[33]

The Connecticut General Assembly responded to the Moravian
Indian petition by setting aside, not granting, the full portion of the
twenty-fifth lot and the lower portion of the twenty-fourth as laid
out by the colony surveyor Roger Sherman for the use of "Gidion an
Indion and Several other Indians living on ye Country Lands…"[34]

The clear intent of the General Assembly was to lay out land
only for the use of the petitioning group (Gideon and several
Indians), that is, the Moravian community, not the general non-
Christian Indian population. They were not parties to the petition
nor did Mauwee have any authority over them. This emerging
community had for the first time its own recognized land base. On
this land base, they constructed their first permanent structure, a
chapel (1752). In addition Mauwee, with the concurrence of the
missionaries, improved a 120-acre land parcel and following
colonial practice equally divided this parcel and allotted a division
to each convert family.[35] This action was taken in clear contrast to
the traditional tribal lineage-based structure of both the Potatuck and
Mahican tribes. By 1752, the Moravian community—the ancestral
group of the present-day Schaghticoke—had clearly shed any past
tribal community and political structure along with its attendant
ideological beliefs. Its ideology was Christian; its liturgy and ritual
was that of the Moravian Church. The community was not of one
tribal ancestry. Its political leadership was non-Indian. It lacked a
land base of its own. It was neither Potatuck nor Mahican, nor the
continuation of any tribal organization. This community was
certainly not a tribe.

An interesting question emerges from this research. If in fact there was a tribe at Schaghticoke, which one of the two separate communities was the tribe? Was it the small, organized convert community or was it the larger non-convert group? It is not disputable that the two were socially, ideologically and politically distinct and separate.

Chapter Seven

The Schaghticoke Community in Transition: 1760-1770

"I shall soon go to the savior now"

Gideon Mauwee died on January 28, 1760 at age 73. He had been a member of the Moravian community for seventeen years. Mauwee appeared to have been gradually ceding his role as the community's steward to his son Josua. Was this a family dynasty in the making or was it that Josua happened to be the most qualified?

Josua had been assisting the Moravians as their linguistic translator since 1752. He was a competent translator of both English and German. As early as 1756, Josua, on the behalf of the community, petitioned the General Assembly.[1] In this memorial, Josua noted that the petition was being submitted:

> ...In behalf of ourselves and our absent Bretern viz. Gideon Mawchu, Martin Roger, Petrus Sherman, Christian Sherman, Salomon, Sherry, Lucas Cooksen, Philippius Sockonok, Paulus Choker, Johannes Peny, Jonathan Worbs, Johannes Worbs, Gornop, Tomaseet...[2]

Yet the records are silent regarding a formal elevation in status. During January of 1759, Josua was finally appointed constable and steward for the community.[3] During August of 1761, he was also held responsible for its moral conditions.[4] Further evidence of his leadership role was a reminder given to him by Martin Mack that he was supposed to be like a "father" among his fellow Christians[5] and that he was responsible for supervising the congregation during the missionary's absence.[6] Like his father before him, for his beliefs and his efforts, Josua was beaten up by hostile non-community Indians (April 1762).[7] Like his father before him, his political influence and status were limited to the Moravian convert community.

Yet significant changes and problems emerged which ultimately brought about an end to the Moravian mission at Schaghticoke. The day prior to his death, Mauwee asked that the men of the community join him for his last instructions. At this final gathering, he stated:[8]

> Bretheren, I shall soon go to the savior now, be very peaceful with one another and love one another, don't argue about the land, rather each of you keep what he has, help one another.

Mauwee's last instructions belied an underlying tension within the community, competition and friction within the community for suitable agricultural land. His son Josua's 1756 petition to the General Assembly reflected a further concern about this issue over reservation land. Josua's 1756 petition provoked the General Assembly in 1757 into appointing for the first time a colony overseer (Jabez Swift). Swift was responsible for both the Christian and non-Christian Indian communities at Schaghticoke.[9]

The role of the colony-appointed overseer over Indians evolved out of the function of the town overseer of the poor. When ordered by the town selectmen with concurrence of a justice of the peace, an indigent or incompetent individual became a ward of the town. The overseer's responsibility was for the care and management of the individual and his or her estate. This individual cannot purchase or sell his estate without the overseer's permission. The overseer was to manage the property and estate of his ward for the best interests of the town and the individual. The aim was to make the individual a productive member of the community, to the point where the individual was no longer a financial burden to the town. In 1725, the colony assumed that responsibility for Indians residing on reserves. One immediate consequence of Swift being appointed overseer of the Schaghticoke reservation was that for the first time both Indian communities were united under a single political authority. The problem was, he was not an Indian but an individual representing the legal jurisdiction of the colony of Connecticut. There was to be no political autonomy for the Schaghticoke as a people.

Further evidence of the community's acculturation to colonial norms was the election in January of 1760, at Swift's prompting of three of the community's men (Samuel, Jeremias, and Salomon) to positions of tythingmen and overseer of the fences for the community.[10] These tythingmen also acted as community assistant constables in association with both the community constable and the town constable of Kent.[11] Swift was introducing the concept of democratically electing officials and instituting positions comparable with a colonial town, as well as ensuring that colonial legal jurisdiction was present. The reservation's legal system became integrated to that of the local town of Kent and the Colony.

What was becoming apparent was that this jurisdictional authority of both town and colony officials was coming into direct conflict with the religious political authority of the Moravian missionaries. At a community conference held on November 16 1760, the Moravian Indian membership noted that the introduction of such public offices into the Moravian community was having an effect that was considered by the Moravians to be harmful to "harmonious life."[12] In other words, colonial jurisdiction was presenting a challenge to the political authority of the Moravian missionaries. It does not take a rocket scientist to figure out who would prevail. This was only one aspect of the problems facing the Moravian community during this time.

Rival Communities

The continued presence of an unstable non-Christian Indian community also presented a similar threat. The Moravian records for this period continually noted incidents involving the actions of this group, including all-night drinking parties, fights, and other disturbances.[13] These incidents also included physical conflicts with outside non-Christian Indian groups such as those from "Wanachquaticok" in Sharon.[14]

In 1761, another source of conflict for the Moravian community appeared in the form of Indian deserters and discharged veterans from the colonial forces in the aftermath of the French and Indian War. The Moravians were a pacifistic organization. They steadfastly attempted to prevent its members from joining the colonial army. Those who did were excluded from the community. (There were at least ten who did enlist from the Schaghticoke community. See Appendix F). Their return and the appearance of other non-affiliated Indians through 1762 created "scandalous scenes."[15] Responding to these pressures, the Moravian community held a council on September 28, 1761 with the intent of "restoring order and discipline" in the community.[16] This was a clear indication of the negative effect these returnees were having on the social cohesion of the convert community. It didn't work. The Moravians were forced to resort to their political competitors for assistance. Four months later, at the request of the community, the local town constable called a meeting at which the reading of the Connecticut "provincial laws" was performed.[17] Thus, the Moravians ceded their authority to that of the colony.

The Moravian community population also underwent a significant transformation during this period. From a 1751 community population of eighty-seven,[18] this community had declined over a ten-year-period to pre-1749 levels. There were fourteen members in 1761/62.[19] A 1762 census of the town of Kent reported an Indian population of 127 persons. The non-Moravian Indian community outnumbered the convert community by 113 persons. The decline continued. By April of 1763 the number of Moravian communicants had decreased down to twelve.[20] The decrease in the number of Moravian converts did not necessarily convert into a loss for the Moravian Church. Many of these converts at Schaghticoke migrated to other Moravian communities in Pennsylvania, Ohio and eventually to Moraviantown in Canada. By 1765, the gross number of Indians at Schaghticoke had decreased to 102.[21] During January of 1774, the Connecticut state census for Kent noted that this population's gross number further decreased to sixty-two (twenty-nine males, thirty-three females). In 1786, (see Appendix G) a total of seventy-one was given, of which twenty were children.

In addition, as early as 1760, the Moravian mission records of the community noted that they were being crowded out of their hunting grounds by the increasing size of the neighboring colonial population.[22] In October of 1762, reports indicated that hunting, a critical subsistence source for the community, was still bringing poor results.[23] In an attempt to counterbalance this decline in subsistence hunting (March 1762), the missionaries stressed that the convert community must place a greater emphasis on agricultural production, especially corn growing. The following year (June 1763), the missionaries were complaining that the farm work was being done carelessly.[24] Gone was the community's ideological drive to succeed. There was one possible cause for this situation.

In 1766, despite the efforts of Jabez Swift the Schaghticoke overseer, alcohol abuse in the non-convert community continued to generate violence and disorder upon the entire reservation population.[25] This situation was aggravated by the continual sale of intoxicants to the Indians by the outside non-Indian population and the inability of the non-Christian Indian community to exert internal influence to stem its use. Josua himself was mentioned as having succumbed to the malady.

In May of 1765, the remaining members of the community petitioned the Moravian elders at Bethlehem for permission to remove to the Wyalusing mission in Pennsylvania. No further action appeared to have been taken on this request. By 1767 there appeared to be a split within the convert community, with some of the community desiring to remove to Pennsylvania, which resulted in a second petition in April of 1767 asking the Moravian Elders for permission to remove to the Friedenshutten mission. In June, the community was informed that corn had been planted there in anticipation of their arrival. Samuel and a number of other community members did leave. In turn, those converts remaining at Schaghticoke petitioned the Connecticut General Assembly (under Josua [Job] Mauwee's name) in May of 1767 asking that the reservation lands be sold by the colony and that the funds from this sale be made available to them so that they could join the Christian Indian community at Stockbridge. The Stockbridge mission was operated by the Society for the Propagation of the Gospel, not by the Moravians.[26] This request in and of itself may have been a reflection of the Moravians' waning influence over this segment of the convert population remaining at Schaghticoke. Despite the concurrence of Jabez Swift, their colony-appointed overseer, their request was denied by the General Assembly. Due to this situation the last Moravian missionary (Thorp) was recalled to Bethlehem in September of 1770, thus ending the Moravian mission's activities at Schaghticoke. Secularization had supplanted Moravian spirituality. What becomes clear is that the Schaghticoke community was neither the continuation of an historic tribe nor was it a continuation of the Moravian mission population.

Indian remnants from numerous tribes had coalesced into two distinct reservation communities at Schaghticoke. One community acquired a distinct spiritual-based ideology and social mores. It was led by non-Indians. The colony of Connecticut set aside lands upon which this community could reside.

What about the "other" community? We know little of them. We have a good idea of their numbers through time; we know that this population was highly transient; we also know that it had little social cohesion or internal political control. The historical record is silent in regards to a leader of the secular community.

It was the colony of Connecticut that brought this situation under control. The appointment of a colony-appointed overseer brought the entire Indian population at Schaghticoke under a single political authority for the first time since 1749 when the Mahican sachem Stephen departed for Bethlehem. But despite the overseer's efforts and intentions, the reservation population spiraled down into the hellish realm of social anomie.

Chapter Eight

Consolidation and Constraints: 1771-1794

Decline

Out of the mission's demise an apparent condition of both social and political discord reigned on the reservation. During this time, the appointment of Jabez Swift as overseer facilitated the emergence of a single secularized Indian community that consisted of the remnants or descendants of both the former mission community along with those of the remaining non-Christian Indian community. Out of this discord, there rose a new reservation-based community leadership. The names of the signatories on a 1771 petition to the General Assembly attest to this.[1] This document contained names associated with both the former Christian and non-Christian communities: Sherman, Warrups, Tobe, Mauwee, Sucknuck and Cocksure. The first signatory was Daniel Sharman. Josua Mauwee's name was not present; Jacob Mauwee, a non-convert was. Thus, initially the Moravian-linked Mauwee name was not associated with the new community's leadership. In this new situation, Josua Mauwee did not continue his family's community leadership role.

In this 1771 petition, as well as a second one submitted the same year, the first signatory was Daniel Sharman. Sharman (Sherman) was the son of Petrus Sherman, a Moravian convert, brother to Chere the last sachem at Potatuck and son of Wereamaug, the last sagamore of the Potatuck tribe. The following year (October 1772), Daniel Mauwee appeared for the first time as the community's principal signatory.[2] He did so again the following year (August and October of 1773).[3] Though the political structure of this new emerging community appeared to be in flux, the Mauwee family name began to reappear in a consistent leadership role.

Unity

In contrast to the apparent social and political helplessness of its predecessor communities, this new community began to take steps to address problems associated with the integrity of the reservation boundaries (October 1771).[4] The result was the appointment of a new overseer (Elisha Swift). When Swift resigned to relocate to the Susquehanna territory in Pennsylvania, the community leadership quickly petitioned for and recommended a replacement (Ruben Swift, October 1772). When Swift died the following year, the community, led by Daniel Mayhew (also Jacob Rogers, Benjamin Warrups, Samuel Cockshure, Jeremiah Cockshure, Peter Kehor, Jonas Cockshure, Job Sucknuck, and Robert Moses), again petitioned for a replacement[5] (Abraham Fuller, 1773). The reservation community, whether consciously or not, realized the need for the protection and guidance of a state-appointed overseer. It was also a strong testament to the presence of a dependency relationship between these Indians and the Connecticut authorities. The Schaghticoke as a community could not stand alone.

"a needy indolent people"

According to a 1774 colony census, the town of Kent had a total Indian population of sixty-two, of whom twenty-three were adults (eleven males/thirteen females) and thirty-eight non-adults (age twenty was used as an adult baseline in the survey). It is apparent that this sixty-two-person community was now being represented by a community political authority. Yet, in 1775, despite the presence of Indian community leadership, the Schaghticoke overseer described the community as "a needy indolent people."[6]

In the aftermath of a "meating held by the Indians in Scatecock," a petition to the Connecticut General Assembly was presented in April of 1786.[7] Joseph Mauwee was the principal signatory on the behalf of the community. The petition contained a number of requests from the community (a school, direct payments from the overseer's fund, enforcement of perceived Indian hunting and fishing rights). This petition was a clear indication that a community political authority was present, though it was not autonomous given it was under the supervision of a state-appointed overseer. Yet significantly, the Schaghticoke leadership was trying to assert itself over the overseer. By trying to control the disbursements from the overseer's fund, they were trying to gain a degree of political autonomy. It portended a power struggle between Swift and the community leadership. It was not to be. Fuller, in his capacity as overseer, was the direct representative of the state's sovereignty and jurisdiction over the reservation and its residents. As long as an Indian was resident on these lands, he or she was subject to his authority. This fact alone provided an inducement for many to leave the reservation and become part of surrounding communities.

What was clear is that this community leadership was acting in concert with the Schaghticoke community on its behalf for its betterment. Yet by May of 1792, the Schaghticoke overseer, Abraham Fuller, was noting:

> ...that said Indians are a People almost given up to Drunkeness and Idleness Spending their Time in Stroaling about from place to place in Pursuit of Spirituous Licquor and often Intocsicated with Licquor Lying out Exposed to Dues and Rains and by means of their Imprudence Subject to often Infermities and Deseases and Sickness and Deaths have been frequent Among them for about these five years....[8]

In 1783, Abraham Fuller petitioned the Connecticut General Assembly for permission to sell off some of the reservation lands, the proceeds of which would be used to support the reservation's needy residents.[9] This was a common practice by the state. As Indian populations declined on a reservation, the state as the owner would sell off excess acreage, and the profits from the sale would be used for the support of the remaining reservation residents. Permission was granted for this sale.[10] Forty acres of land were approved for sale by the Assembly. These lands were not sold until December of 1785.[11]

In his 1789 Schaghticoke census, Ezra Stiles[12] noted that Peter Mauwee claimed to be "King" of the Schaghticoke, despite the fact he was younger than seven of his male community members. In that same document (see Appendix H), Stiles noted that the community at that time consisted of sixty-seven individuals. By 1799 Peter

Mauwee along with his wife Eliza (Warrups) were no longer residing at Schaghticoke but were now accepted inhabitants and residing on land as owners in fee in the town of Cornwall, Connecticut,[13] a good day's travel from Schaghticoke. There is no documentary evidence of his acting in the capacity of a community leader acting for or on the behalf of the Schaghticoke reservation community. This view is supported by the fact that Stiles's journal for the day he recorded the tribal list indicated that he was visiting his own lands in Cornwall. Stiles noted that there were four Schaghticoke families in residence in Cornwall. His journal indicated that he did not go near Schaghticoke or the town of Kent.

The last interaction between this community and the Connecticut General Assembly for the next twelve years (until 1799) was a May 1787 petition of Joseph Mauwee asking that a non-Indian individual be provided to plow their lands as they were incapable of doing it themselves.[14] Out of sixty-seven individuals, not one was capable of plowing a field. This request suggests a very dysfunctional on-reservation community. Contemporaneously, in her biographical sketch,[15] Eunice Mauwee, a surviving granddaughter of Gideon Mauwee noted "They did not cultivate the land, but rather, worked for anyone who would have them." This was a far different situation from the time of her grandfather Gideon Mauwee, who as she noted:

> …governed as he planned telling them when to sow and where, when and how to gather crops, He allowed no drinking. The tribe flourished under him and scattered after him.

During this period, the only concern with the state that involved any Schaghticoke was in May 1799.[16] Peter Mauwee petitioned the state over his wife's (Eliza [Warrups] Mauwee) inherited non-reservation estate in Kent. That very same month (May 1799), the General Assembly also received a petition from the Schaghticoke community. As in the 1786 petition, this one was the result of a "Meting of the Natives…" in which they asked that no further reservation lands be sold to pay off debts accumulated by members of the Schaghticoke community.[17] The principal signatory to this document was, as in 1786, Joseph, not Peter Mauwee the purported "King." The other signatories in order of signing were John Peters,

Peter Sherman, Daniel Sucknucks, Elihu Mauwee, Isaack Sucknucks, Job Sucknucks, Danielson Mauwee, Abraham Kunkapot, Levi Succonnucks, Peter Mauwee, and Jonas Cocshure. Their petition was declined.

It appears that both political authority and concerted community action was sporadic in nature. The community itself demonstrated no concerted economic or social activities during this period. Things were falling apart.

The internal effectiveness of Schaghticoke political authority was limited by the nature (overseer) and type of relationship (dependency) between the reservation community and the state of Connecticut. That is one of dominance and dependency, not self-determination. Yet with the Schaghticoke, the initial appearance of an overseer unified the reservation population for the first time since 1749 when the Mahican sachem Stephen departed with his wife for Bethlehem, Pennsylvania. But there was also a downside.

The downside of this relationship between this Schaghticoke Indian community and Connecticut became readily apparent in 1775 when, as a result of a conflict between John and David Sherman and the resulting injury sustained by John, the state's full arbitrary authority over this community and its leaders was expressed:

> that David Sherman, the Indian that wounded his brother, be assigned in service to defray the expense incurred by wounding his brother; which report is accepted and approved...and that said Samuel Canfield Esqr be & he is hereby appointed & authorised to asign in service the said David Sherman for the satisfaction of such part of the expense, as has arisen on account of wounding his Brother..."[18]

No hearing, no court trial, no chance to offer a defense. David Sherman is bound over to an attorney by the General Assembly who will hire him off to others to work off the costs of his brother's care.

All this was a result of an overseer's communication. Why? The Indian overseer, as with his town counterpart, the overseer of the poor, had, by virtue of his appointment, the authority to do so. How did this authority come about?

In the same resolve issued by the General Assembly, the issue of the proper use of reservation lands was also addressed:

> And it is thereupon resolved by this Assembly, that Majr. Samuel Canfield Esq., and Capt. Sherman Boardman be and they are hereby appointed a committee, who are hereby impowered to make a new allotment of Said Lands to the Several Indians as shall be necessary for their support, and the Residue the overseer of said Indians is hereby directed to lease out for the purpose of Defraying the expenses of said Sickness and the Avail thereof over & above after repairing & making necessary fences, said Overseer shall render an Account to the Genl Assembly.

Is it any wonder that a coherent viable community political leadership could never become entrenched at Schaghticoke? The state's focus was upon the betterment of the individual ward, not upon groups. The state entertained no notion of working through a community political structure. It must be understood that Indians living on a reserve such as Schaghticoke were not considered to be residents of the colony, by virtue of not having attained a settlement in any town within the colony. Herein lies the critical distinction that resulted in the state asserting such authority over the reservation Schaghticoke. They were liminal indigent peoples. They had no rights as citizens, nor were they liable for taxes. During the colonial era they had the protection of English law. The same rules applied to any other person in similar circumstances, regardless of his race, who had not gained a town settlement. This concept was a carry-over from English feudalism,[19] wherein outside of the cities, a person not belonging to a Lord's manor[20] had no rights or protections; nor were they subject to any taxation or obligations imposed on the manor's tenant population. These people were vulnerable and often ill-treated, not only by the settled populace but also by the courts. In New England, the town supplanted the manor as the focus of residence and identity. It was the source of protection, the focus of obligations. Like the manor, the town was the locus of socialization. Those not part of it were considered "others," somehow different. The intensity of these feelings in the towns of colonial Connecticut cannot be understated. Within this context, understanding a town's attitude towards a neighboring Indian reservation and its indigent occupants does not require much imagination.

The state's stringent control of the reservation population, like that of the feudal manor, inhibited initiative. The state's intentions were not malevolent. The state's goal was noteworthy just like Indian reservations on the Federal level (and also state welfare agencies). The goal of both efforts was known, but the means to attaining it were grossly misguided. In both cases, all that was accomplished was the continuation of abject poverty and a social system that promoted despair and self-devaluation.

Thus, the state's actions towards her Indian populations had to be understood within the context of the state's historical heritage. This heritage can be directly linked to the role and authority of the overseer of the poor. Habitation, be it as a tenant of the manor or an admitted inhabitant of a town, was the essential component for gauging one's standing. Without it, one was a vagrant, an outliver, an indigent. Towns expelled them or "warned" them off. Under English and natural law, such an expulsion of Indians from the colony would have been illegal. The answer: set aside reservations for such indigent peoples. Place them under the colony's guardianship like the manorial Lord over his tenants, and turn them into productive residents. Connecticut's attitude was to reform such people in the process, turning them into contributing residents instead of being a drain on the public treasury for their support. Towns maintained similar reserves. They called them "poor farms."

Connecticut's historical position towards the application of poor laws towards indigent people regardless of ethnicity must also be understood. These laws were not Indian laws. They covered all individuals. In 1719 the colony enacted, "An Act for the relieving and ordering of Idiots, impotent, diftracted, and idle Perfons."[21] This law formed the basis of Connecticut's poor laws.[22] Within the body of this poor law can be found a process of application that addresses indigent persons. Nowhere within the text of this poor law is mentioned the word Indian. Its application was based solely upon the subject person's socio-economic standing. But it did apply to them when necessary.[23]

An overseer's authority over his appointed wards was substantial. All the affairs of his wards were subject to his approval; that was his mandate, to manage the affairs of such people, as they were deemed incapable of managing their own.

So Sherman's injury resulted in significant medical costs which neither Sherman nor the community had the ability to pay. The assets they had were the individual land allotments instituted by Gideon Mauwee that those descendants of the Moravian community still maintained. The General Assembly responded by ordering a committee to investigate the situation of the Schaghticoke community.[24] They recommended that the present land allotments be disbanded and new allotments made for the "few" remaining (forty to fifty) Indians. The remaining lands were to be leased out to non-Indians and the proceeds were to be used to support the expenses incurred by the remaining Indians.

As an indication of the state of affairs on the reservation, the General Assembly also directed that a portion of the monies derived from the leases be used to repair or replace the boundary fences enclosing the reservation.[25] The lack of fence maintenance is indicative of a lack of economic activity, namely farming and animal husbandry. This supports Eunice Mauwee's comments noted earlier concerning the lack of such activities by the Schaghticoke community.

In one single action, the General Assembly demonstrated how ineffectual any attempt at developing a reservation community's government would be. Though the Schaghticoke's post-Revolutionary War population remained stable,[26] sixty-seven individuals in 1789,[27] their demographic, community, social and economic situation did not. Abraham Fuller, their overseer, described their plight in May 1792:[28]

> ...that said Indians are a People almost given up to Drunkeness and Idleness Spending their Time strouling about from place to place in Persuit of Spiritous Liquors and often Intocksicated with Licquor Lying out exposed to ____ and Rains and by means of their imprudence Subject often to Infirmities and Diseases and Sickness and Death have been Frequent among Them for about these Five Years passed...

It appears by this observation that community leadership was ineffectual and lacked widespread community support. There also appeared not to be any community consensus as to standards of behavior and a means to enforce them other than sanctions imposed by the overseer.

"It never recovered...."

By the combination of both internal and external enabling factors, a single Schaghticoke community did emerge in the mid 1770s. Yet a competing set of external political factors constrained the elaboration and enlargement of the community to that of a post-contact tribal entity. The political dominance of the state via a developing dependency relationship as well as state political dominance constrained political development and community social identity. Another factor was the demographic repercussions from the War of Independence. According to Eunice Mauwee, many of the community's men enlisted in the Continental Army, "some died and the survivors never returned...The war was a severe blow to the tribe...It never recovered...."[29] The social bonds within the community were apparently weak. The historical records of this period give no indication of the presence of any community-based ideology that would have fostered a group identity that would have bound an individual to the community. In other words, these men felt that there was nothing worth coming home to. The loss of this essential male age cohort became a critical factor in the post-1800 era. Stiles's 1789 Schaghticoke census clearly shows a missing 16-30 year old male cohort (see Appendix H). There was an available female marriage pool, but the lack of a corresponding male component forced female ethnic and geographical out-marriages leading to their subsequent dispersal into the surrounding communities and states. The net result was a severe population decline in the 1800s as well as voids in the leadership roles normally ascribed to adult males.

Summary

If an argument were to be made for when a single unified community emerged which ultimately became what has been commonly referred to as the Schaghticoke Tribe, the period between 1771 and 1775 would be the timeframe for this emergence. A single political authority representing a single Indian communal entity acting in concert on its own behalf appeared for the first time at Schaghticoke during this time period. Yet, as we have seen, this development was short-lived.

Prior to this time Schaghticoke consisted of two conflicting multi-ethnic remnant communities that were socially, politically and to a large degree culturally separate from one another. One was large, amorphous with no definable ideological, political or social structure. By appearances, this community lacked and offered no social, hence psychological stability. Being unstable, its population was highly transient.

The other was minuscule in comparison to the first. Yet it had structure, internal cohesion, self-identification, direction and, most importantly, stability. Yet neither had control over the other. It was by the concerted actions of this small stable community that a permanent land base was set aside for the Indians' use by the colony of Connecticut. Yet, despite this, the leadership roles of Gideon and Josua Mauwee held no sway outside of the smaller Moravian Indian community. It lacked the political and social authority to do so. It was a liminal minority in relation to the larger community.

Technically the lands were still part of traditional Mahican tribal territory. The Mahican sachem for the area, Waasampa (Stephen), was himself a Moravian convert. His sympathies were toward his religious brethren at Schaghticoke. Schaghticoke, during this period, was a place name, not a people, definitely not a tribe as understood by the national government of the time.[30]

The Moravian Indian community at Schaghticoke did not represent a social or political continuum of the historic Potatuck tribe. Both structurally and ideologically, they were different. Portions of the Potatuck tribe dispersed into individual and family fragments in the face of acculturative, spatial and political pressures that began with the first sustained historical contact with a non-

Indian culture (Woodbury, circa 1673). Yet at the same time, a significant portion of the Potatuck remained socially and politically intact long after the appearance of an Indian community at Schaghticoke.

The appearance of a Moravian community at Schaghticoke (circa 1749) was ultimately a responsive adaptation by dispersed detribalized fragments. In or during this psychologically destabilizing fragmentation process, some of these fragmented Indians joined and intermarried with members of the Mahican tribe; others affiliated themselves with the Mahican village communities at Shecomeko and Wequanach. Others joined the Housatonic-Stockbridge communities in Massachusetts, the Oneida Iroquois, or the polyglot Indian settlement at Schaghticoke, New York.

After settling at these differing locales, some of these expatriates came in contact with a new and potentially stabilizing ideology in the form of the Moravian Church. Many of these diverse Indians joined the missions established by the Moravians. There they adopted and shared a new ideology and self-identity. The Moravian community at Schaghticoke was an example of this process at work. At Schaghticoke, this community shared the lands with non-convert tribal remnants that oftentimes discriminated against their Moravian neighbors.

By 1770, as a result of the continual depopulation at Schaghticoke, the smallness of the numbers of both communities, the appearance of a colony-appointed overseer, and the disappearance of the constraining/separatist effects of the Moravian missionaries, a temporary favorable social and political environment was created that enabled both communities to merge. Along with their small population, the apparent chaotic social situation on the reservation also facilitated this unifying process. In order to address this situation and to address land issues with neighboring non-Indian landowners, the Schaghticoke in 1772 petitioned that an overseer be appointed by the colony to look after their welfare.[31] What the Schaghticoke did not understand was that the role of a colony-appointed overseer was not only to be their advocate but also to manage and overseer the affairs of his appointed wards.[32] Such wards were deemed incapable of managing their own affairs. The presence of such an overseer represented a complete antithesis to the

internal community process of evolving political leadership and
social unity. His presence and traditional role, while well intended,
kept the physical community together, but actually in the long run
worked against the wards' self-sufficiency. There was an exception,
but this lay years down the road.

It was at this time that Schaghticoke became a people and ceased
being a place. In 1776, the state of Connecticut had reservation
lands surveyed and allotted to each individual or family.[33] The
people inhabiting this place began acting as a singular community
under one political authority acting at the behest of the community.
Yet, what could have happened didn't. The advent of the colony
overseer in conjunction with one of the unanticipated consequences
of the American Revolution—the loss to the Schaghticoke
community of an entire generation of males who should have
emerged as the next generation of community leaders—were to
have near fatal consequences for the community. As Eunice
Mauwee insightfully observed, the Schaghticoke never recovered
from this loss. Though at least eight adult males remained on the
reservation after 1800, none was willing to assume any leadership
responsibilities. Why was this so?

In 1798, Timothy Dwight, the President of Yale University,
passed through the town of Kent and made the following
observations of the Schaghticoke reservation lands and its
occupants:

> The land is naturally excellent, is miserably cultivated, both
> by the Indians and their tenants...To these objects very
> affecting and melancholy additions were made by the
> wigwams, sixteen in number, by the degraded appearance of
> their woman and children....[34]

Yet despite this lack of political leadership, and the degraded
conditions on the reservation, the community at Schaghticoke did
persist. To whom did they owe this persistence and survival as a
community?

Chapter Nine

A New Century Begins: 1801-1841

Mr. Beach's Account Book

In April of 1801, the Indian overseer of the Schaghticoke reservation, Abraham Fuller, noted the condition of the Indian community under his wardship:

…At the time this tract was reserved for the use of the Indians their number was about one hundred & fifty, many were industrious, active men But even then they actually cultivated and improved but a small proportion of the land fit for cultivation The number of Indians has been gradually decreasing, and at this time, including persons of every description belonging to the tribe, amounts to no more than thirty five These are without exception, addicted to intoxication & idleness in ___ extreme ____ and are adverse to every kind of labour They are not in general attempt to cultivate more than six acres of land in a year, & this they manage in a very negligent manner From their habits of living they have been for several years past much afflicted with sickness then formerly, and the expenses of making necessary provision for them, have been consequently encreased The lands which the Indians do not cultivate, although let out & managed to the best advantage under the circumstances, produce but a partial provision for defraying these expenses: Being in a situation to be let from year to year, & under the incumberence of the Indians residing on any part they choose, the lands are daily becoming of less value; the fences are much decayed, and fifteen pounds per year is the most that can be obtained for the use of the lands From these circumstances a debt of one hundred & twenty pounds has already accrued and the rent of the lands is in no wise adequate to the payment of the interest on the debt, &

furnishing necessaries for those Indians who are unable to furnish themselves[1]

When compared to Ezra Stiles's 1789 Schaghticoke community census that totaled "...67 Souls...,"[2] we find that during a twelve-year period only slightly more that half the 1789 population remained. Most importantly, Fuller's depiction of the state of the Schaghticoke community was devoid of any evidence of community leadership and any concerted community actions in maintaining and cultivating reservation lands. The presence of "...intoxication and idleness...." belies the non-presence of either kin-group based social constraints common to Indian society, or the power to apply tradition forms of social sanctions to rectify serious social and economic issues. It is also indicative of a misguided state policy towards the state's reservation populations.

"as will give therefor the highest price"

Despite the presence of abundant land suitable for cultivation in 1801, only six acres of reservation land were being used for agriculture. That translates into a little more that one acre of land in production for every 5.8 members of the community, well below a level necessary to sustain this community for a full year's subsistence cycle. It was no wonder that the number of ill persons within the reservation population was increasing. This situation, despite the presence of sufficient natural resources, demonstrated the Schaghticoke community's inability to exploit the reservation's natural resources and to internally address community problems without outside intervention of the overseer.

On the individual level, reservation lands allotted to individual persons were being rented out to non-Indians. This practice began around 1785 as a means to provide support for the reservation's residents.[3] Rather than relying upon themselves as a community to subsist, the reservation population became more and more dependent upon the state, more specifically, their need to have the state-appointed overseer provide an increasing amount of essential assistance. This was not the state's intended goal. The problem is the same today as it was in 1801. The more the state intervenes in the life of a community, the more that community becomes dependent upon the state and not itself.

In 1801, in an effort to erase the accumulative debt of the reservation's residents, to improve their condition, and to provide a continual source of funding for their support, the General Assembly authorized another sale of reservation lands "to sell, & by Deed convey to such Person or Persons as will give therefor the highest price."[4]

During the course of his many journeys (circa 1794), Yale President Timothy Dwight[5] had occasion to visit many Indian communities throughout New England and New York. As a result, he was familiar with such Indian settlements and thus could render distinctive qualitative judgments on them and their condition. He quite correctly noted that the lands at Schaghticoke were good, but poorly utilized. Expert utilization of land for agricultural use by the Indians was no strange occurrence. Its poor use was. Such a poor land usage would imply both a lack of leadership within the community and a lack of will for self-reliance. For the size of the Schaghticoke community, there were ample bottomlands, especially those on the alluvial flood plains bordering on the Housatonic River, useful for both domestic and commercial agricultural production. The community seemed to lack the will and organization to undertake such an activity. The Schaghticoke community had hit rock bottom.

Adding to this situation was the resignation in May of 1801 of Abraham Fuller as their overseer. In its October 1801 session, the Connecticut General Assembly appointed Abel Beach of the town of Kent to replace Fuller in that capacity as the overseer or conservator of the Indian community at Schaghticoke.[6] Beach was to hold this position as overseer until his death in 1853, a total of fifty-two years. During this entire time, he maintained an account book.[7] (See Appendix H) This record gives us the only continuous first-hand depiction of the Schaghticoke community during this period.

A Stagnated Community

In his records from 1801 to 1820, Abel Beach cited a total of fifty-two adults associated with the Indian settlement at Schaghticoke.[8] Out of this number, eight of the eleven 1799 Schaghticoke political leaders remained for varying periods on the reservation; others just simply disappeared. Those remaining eight cited in Beach's records were:

John Cockshure: He was present at Schaghticoke in 1801 and 1802. He was residing in Dutchess County, New York when he died in 1807.

Joseph Mauwee: "Joe." He was on the reservation in 1803. He was living off the reservation in 1810. He was residing with his family in the town of Warren, Connecticut, where he died (1813).

Peter Sherman: In 1801 he was residing in Dover, New York. He was still there in 1806. He died at Dover, New York in 1812.

John Peters: "Old John." He was residing on the reservation in 1806. He died there in 1809.

Daniel Sucknuck: He was on the reservation in 1806. He died there in 1813.

Peter Mauwee: He was on the reservation between 1806-1809. He died there in 1822.

Elihu Mauwee: He died on the reservation in 1809.

Job Sucknux: He was on the reservation in 1811. He died there in 1820.

Thus at least two of the eight were still present through 1820. In theory they should have continued to have exercised some political authority within the community. Unfortunately, during this time, Beach's records indicate this was not the case. The lack of contemporaneous petitions from the Schaghticoke community to the state supports this conclusion.

"...Resolved by this Assembly"

As a result of this community inaction, commonplace community activities and responsibilities fell upon Beach to fulfill. The demands on the Schaghticoke fund created the need for additional reservation land sales. These sales grew in proportion to the community's increasing demands. The only answer to this problem was continued state authorized sales of reservation lands:[9]

> ...Resolved by this Assembly, that said Abel Beach be, & he is hereby authorized & empowered to sell the aforesaid tract of Land & to give & execute legal deeds of Conveyance thereof to the Purchaser or Purchasers — & that the monies arising the sale thereof be put at interest for the benefit of said Indians, under the direction of their Overseer, in the same manner as been done with the monies arising from the sale of a part of said sequestered lands heretofore made...

It was a vicious cycle that went unrecognized. The state viewed itself as helping the Schaghticoke out of poverty in the process making them productive inhabitants of the state. By this process, the state unconsciously created a dependency relationship that intensified through time. Beach became the sole figure of authority. He dealt with his wards on an individual basis, not as a community. There was no evidence of any community-based leadership. What had occurred was just the opposite of what was intended. The law of unintended consequences was at work. As noted earlier, at given points in time the demands of this relationship exceeded the funds to support it, which in turn necessitated the need for more sales of state-owned reservation lands to provide additional funding for the relationship. As we shall see, Beach's genius provided a solution to this problem.

Beach's records for this period note that he was left to arrange and provide the necessary materials for the burial of community members, including those who would have been considered to have been community leaders ("boards & nails for coffin," "Winding clothes," "½ pint rum," "½ lb candles," "coffin," "Horses and wagon to cary Corpes to Grave."). No one from the community stepped forward to assist him. Beach's records noted that with the exception of one year (1817), from 1802 through 1820 he personally made arrangements for all the community's burials, providing burial clothing, candles, coffins, rum or brandy (for the cleansing of the body) and transportation and burial of the deceased.

Despite having a sizable land base, and having one, possibly two older Indian cemeteries within its bounds (the Moravian burial ground, and a second used by the non-convert community that was said to have been located on the north-eastern slope of Schaghticoke Mountain), the reservation community did not maintain its own Indian burial ground. Instead, Beach had to make an annual (sometimes bi-annual) payment for cemetery plots out of community funds ("paid Ephraim Beardsley for the use of the Burieing Ground 3.00", to Do for use of Buring ground 1 yr 3.00"). The deceased were interred in the town's South Cemetery on the east side of the Housatonic River opposite the reservation. There was no evidence of community assistance or participation in this most important of social and cultural occasions. The burials appeared to follow the Christian rites. As any notations are lacking, it is presumed that the cleansing and burial shroud wrapping was performed by the deceased's family members. The presence of any community assistance in organizing and leading these activities would have provided some indication for the presence of a political organization or leadership within the community. None was present.

When it came to retrieving ill or injured Schaghticoke community individuals who had taken up residence in surrounding communities, there was no community response. It was up to Beach to arrange for the retrieval. Between 1802 and 1820, Beach arranged for and paid non-Schaghticoke for the retrieval of seventeen ill, injured, or destitute Schaghticoke individuals, not only from surrounding Connecticut communities such as Warren, New Milford and Newtown, but also Dover and Armenia, New York. No assistance was provided to Beach by the Schaghticoke community in these efforts. This is further evidence that there existed no internal authority to direct or influence efforts to assist community members in need. At the same time, Beach's records show that after 1910 there was an increase in retrievals of Schaghticoke living in other non-reservation locations. This represents the fractured nature of the Schaghticoke community, a highly transient community.

Recent research performed by the Bureau of Indian Affairs that analyzed marriage rates within the Schaghticoke community, reflects Beach's data.[10] The contrast was between members of the community marrying one another (endogamy) and those marrying outside the community (exogamy). The endogamic rate is an indicator of community health. The higher the rate, the more socially cohesive the community and the more confidence a community has in itself.

The Bureau found that from 1801 to 1810 the endogamic marriage rate within the Schaghticoke community was 41.7%. Between 1811 and 1820 this rate plummeted to 18.2%. More Schaghticoke were moving out and marrying outside the community after 1810. The community was falling apart. This rate remained low through 1840.

Other information present in the Beach records depicts the inability or unwillingness of the community to assist its own. The overseer throughout this period had to pay outsiders to provide firewood for needy community members ("drawing 3 loads wood for old John & Ann .75," "cutting and drawing wood for Abrigail," "Drawing wood for J Tomuck.") No member of the community stepped forward to assist in this effort, despite the presence of abundant oak, maple and pine trees on the reservation. Beach also had to see to the health and sanitation of community members. Eleven reservation community members had to be placed in non-Indian households in order to obtain adequate care. Surprisingly, he also had to provide non-Indian midwives to assist in on-reservation births ("paid to Mrs Bull for her services as midwife 1.50," "paid Mrs Morey for services as midwife 2.00").

In addition, Beach had to pay out of the Schaghticoke fund he administered to have lands plowed and gardens prepared for community members incapable of or unwilling to do so for themselves ("paid E. Thayer for plowing," "to plowing Sarah's garding .50," "Plowing garden for Eunice & Sarah 1.00"). This necessity in and of itself demonstrates the lack of community cohesion and the non-presence of anyone or any group of individuals capable of creating any community-based action to assist those of their own community, especially the elderly women.

It was also indicative of a lack of adult males within the community who could perform these tasks.

Beach's records reveal only one individual during this period who exhibited any tendency among this community for the betterment of himself and his family. This was Benjamin Chickens, a grandson of Chickens Warrups who at one time possessed two hundred acres of land in fee holding adjacent to the south boundary of the reservation. Benjamin was noted in the Connecticut records as one who worked to improve the family's remaining lands, thus increasing their value.[11] He was also noted in Beach's records as regularly receiving assistance, but as one family head who consistently ensured that his children gained an education ("paid Benj Chickings School Rate," cited continuously 1807-1823). Chickens's efforts though, were directed only towards the betterment of his family, not for the Schaghticoke community. He was paid by Beach for performing services that involved certain community members such as: "paid Benjm Chickens for keeping Mawwee's Child 16 weeks" (April 1814), "paid Benjm Chickings for fetching Eunice & her children from George Bull's to Scatecook" (September 1822). Beach's overseer records as well as those of the state suggest that Chickens and his family lived apart from the Schaghticoke Indian community.

It is apparent that during this 1802-1820 period, Abel Beach was in essence and by default filling the role of community political leader. A nexus of any state-tribe political authority was certainly missing. It is also noteworthy that the only indication of initiative shown by an Indian (Benjamin Chickens) in Beach's records was one that appears not to have been part of the reservation community, but who lived nearby on his own property. Only one reservation community member (Abraham Rice) ensured that his children were educated on a continual basis ("paid for Schooling Abraham Rice's children 3.13").

During this time, the members of the Schaghticoke community appeared to be only marginally self-sufficient. According to Beach's accounts, they maintained gardens that supplied some of their agricultural needs. A limited number of individuals such as Peter Mauwee raised income by selling rye from their allotments ("pd

Peter mauwee for 4 Bushels of Rye @4/6 3.00"). However, these food staples as well as necessary goods, tools and hardware were provided by Beach when the need arose. Foodstuffs were also obtained via the renting of land allotments to townspeople ("By 32 bushels Rye of Richard Lain for rent of land 32.00"). Additionally, under Beach's direction the community appeared to be shifting its dwellings from wigwams to wood structures.[12] Numerous entries appeared in Beach's accounts beginning in 1805, mentioning the drawing and cutting of board wood, construction of dwellings, and subsequent repairs.

Was it any wonder that the Schaghticoke Tribal Nation, in its petition for Federal recognition, could not demonstrate to the BIA the presence of any "tribal" political authority during this 1800-1821 time period? Initially, the BIA tried to claim that the mere presence of a state-appointed overseer was sufficient to prove that the state recognized a tribe at Schaghticoke. This "state" recognition, coupled with falsely contrived endogamic marriage rates, was initially used by the BIA to give the Schaghticoke petitioners a "pass" for recognition. The Interior Board of Indian Appeals (IBIA) rejected this "state recognition" as having no probative value in proving the existence of a tribe. The BIA, in a letter to IBIA after initially recognizing the Schaghticoke Tribal Nation, admitted it "erred" in calculating the marriage rates for the Schaghticoke community. Initially, the BIA claimed that this endogamic marriage rate was above 50% during this period, which would have been sufficient to infer political community. Upon being directed by the Secretary of the Interior to recalculate this rate using the BIA's own traditional methodology, the rate between 1811 and 1820, as we noted earlier, was 18.2%.

A Pattern Continues: 1821-1841

The same pattern of overseer activities present between 1802 and 1820 continued through 1841. Based upon Beach's records there appeared to be no political activity, such as communal actions or self-help initiatives within the Schaghticoke community during this time. There were no communications from this community to the state of Connecticut. The only communication with the state was from the Schaghticoke overseer to the Litchfield County Superior Court in the form of his annual account expenditure reports. These financial statements were required by state statute and did not constitute a political nexus between the state and the reservation community.

Based upon Beach's records, during this period five adult males were frequently present at the reservation who could have assumed a leadership role. They were Benjamin Chickens, Ned Rice, Jacob Mauwee, Taber Mauwee, and Abraham Rice. The overseer records indicate none of them did.

Necessary activities required for the well-being of the Schaghticoke community, in the absence of community leadership, still defaulted to the overseer:

- Providing burial materials, clothing and cemetery plots for the community's deceased members.

- Placing ill community members in on-reservation and off-reservation homes to provide for their care.

- Paying for gardens to be plowed for elderly and invalid community members.

- Providing firewood for elderly community members.

- Providing dwelling repairs for the community elderly and invalids.

- Retrieving ill or destitute community members or kin from other locations or states

- Construction of dwellings for community members.

There is no evidence that Beach worked with the assistance or advice of any community members in carrying out these tasks, tasks which, under normal circumstances, would have included the involvement of a community at the behest of its leadership.

Instead, a significant number of the Schaghticoke resided off the reservation and had to be bought back when ill or destitute at cost, from locations such as Bridgeport, Norwalk, Wethersfield, Litchfield, Warren, Newtown, Sharon, Cornwall and Northville in Connecticut, and Pines Plains in New York. The towns in which these "returnees" were residing did not want to assume the costs and responsibilities for these non-town inhabitants when they became destitute or ill.[13] Instead, they procured town orders to return these individuals to the reservation. Beach as overseer had to comply. Beach also provided funds for one community member to permanently leave (John Suckernuck) for Oneida in New York (1834). This accounted for eleven of the thirty-seven Schaghticoke Beach provided for during this period.

John Barber,[14] in his 1836 observations of the Schaghticoke noted: "A granddaughter of the sachem, Eunice Mauwehu, and two or three families are all that remain of the tribe at Scatacook." Evidently, Beach was administering to a highly transient and dispersed community. Such being the case, like the secular Indian community at Schaghticoke of the mid-1700s, it would seem that this residential instability would be a factor inhibiting the development of the community both politically and economically. There was no community-based leadership. Beach continued to fill this void.

Only three individuals under Beach's care showed any signs of economic activities. Two of these, Benjamin and Nancy Chickens, were able to establish and maintain commercial accounts in the local community beginning in 1823.[15] This clearly shows an integration into the local Kent community. We recall that earlier Benjamin Chickens (Warrups) was engaged by Beach to carry out various tasks for the reservation community. He was also shown to have consistently seen to his children's education. He did not reside on the reservation, but on his own fee-held lands.

The third individual was a reservation resident. This was Jacob Mauwee, a great-grandson of Gideon Mauwee. Beginning in May of 1838, commercial records[16] noted that Jacob was able to establish a credit line and made purchases on a regular basis. These purchases included non-essentials that in turn suggested that Mauwee was producing enough income for discretionary spending. Like Chickens, he was participating in the local economy, breaking free of the reservation's dependency ideology. How did he accomplish this?

Beach's records note that in 1830 Jacob was residing off-reservation with the Martin Preston family. Prior to this time, he was not receiving assistance from Beach. According to the account records, Mauwee took ill and was taken to the reservation to be cared for. This happened a second time during May of 1841. Three years previous (1838), he was not only able to establish a line of credit at the general store belonging to Daniel Morehouse, but he also began doing work for him. By 1842, Jacob and his brother Joseph began to do wage-earning work on a regular basis on the reservation for Abel Beach. Beach had hit on something.

Helping Hands, 1842-1853

Beginning around 1842, a noticeable change occurred in Beach's records. Something was happening within the Schaghticoke community. Not only were services and goods provided more detailed and specific to individuals residing on the reservation, but in 1846 the tempo of community economic activity on the reservation increased. This increase was also reflected in documents in the town of Kent.[17]

According to his account book,[18] from 1840 to 1844 Beach was providing support to only four reservation residents: Jacob Mauwee, the elderly Eunice Mauwee, Julia (Mauwee) Kilson and Elihu Mauwee, essentially one extended family. Jacob as we have seen was a reservation resident until 1840. Throughout this entire period there was a notable decrease in reported mortalities due to the presence of a smaller reservation population and the assimilation of outliving former community members into the mainstream society. On the reservation, community services and support provided by Beach followed the same pattern of activity as noted previously, including sizable amounts of foodstuffs and products for the Indian community purchased from neighboring merchants.

In 1842, Beach's records show that Jacob Mauwee began receiving money and goods from Beach for work performed on the reservation. Such activities performed by Mauwee were butchering, woodcutting, sowing pastures, woodworking, and hoeing corn. That same year Jacob was joined by Joseph Mauwee in these economic activities. In July of 1844, Beach's accounts noted that John Mauwee was also receiving pay for work as a day laborer on the reservation. The reservation community appeared to be turning the corner.

Abel Beach, in a break from past practice, began utilizing reservation members to perform needed tasks on the reservation. No longer did he hire non-reservation labor to do this manual work. There were community members who were now willing to help themselves. They were hired by Beach, assigned tasks by Beach, and were paid by Beach. His sole authority on the reservation remained, but now people residing on the reservation were putting their labor into improving the community and earning a wage to boot (see Appendix I). More and more, the Schaghticoke community began participating in a cash economy. A process of shedding the chains of dependency began. So says Mr. Beach's account book.

Additionally, in July of 1842, Truman Bradley, from the town of Sharon, began to work for Beach. Bradley was the non-Indian (black) husband of Julia (Mauwee) Kilson. She was the daughter of Parmelia Mauwee, a community member. All four men (the three Mauwees and Bradley) received pay and foodstuffs for their work. The following January the three were joined by Alexander V. Kilson, the brother of Julia Kilson. For the next seven years John Mauwee, Truman Bradley, and Alexander Kilson maintained the reservation.[19] The reservation lands produced corn, rye, wheat, hay, and pumpkins. Their labors included butchering, thrashing, repairs and construction, plowing, roadwork, pasturing, haying, basket making and harvesting. They prospered in this work. By 1843, Truman Bradley had opened a line of credit with Lorenzo & Morehouse.[20] Value Kilson opened such a line there in 1847. Truman Bradley, (Alexander) Kilson, Value Kilson and George (Bradley) did the same at Kent Furnace Company in 1851.[21] Both Kilson and Truman also opened a credit line with Asa Slade in 1854.[22] We know from these account books that these men also performed labor off the reservation, which contributed further towards their economic self-reliance.

The efforts and labors of these three men, as noted earlier, were instituted, directed, and paid for by the Indian overseer, not a community political leader. Their labors in part started a reservation-based economy. Other income producing economic activities appeared. The reservation community, especially Eunice Mauwee, was known for its basket making. The account books also mention George Bradley coming to the store to barter baskets made on the reservation. The accounts of Lorenzo & Morehouse noted that during October of 1852 Value Kilson, besides laboring two days for Morehouse and purchasing hay, also purchased ten bushels of apples. Likewise, in 1853, Truman Bradley, besides being paid cash for labors performed for Morehouse, on October 1 purchased fifteen bushels of apples. The volume purchased suggests that both Value Kilson and Truman Bradley were supplementing their individual incomes by producing hard cider and selling it on the open market. This practice is still commonplace around the township of Kent. In a similar vein, Value Kilson's abnormally high purchasing pattern of sugar and molasses suggests that Kilson was also supplementing his income by running a still. This practice was not unknown on the reservation. Accounts of the later annual reservation "Rattlesnake Hunts" mention the presence and use of "Sagwa" circa 1880-1919. This potent "cure," euphemistically referred to as an "antidote for rattlesnake bites," was produced on the reservation.

Another important sign of community improvement has also been noted. Marriage rates within the community increased dramatically after 1841. As noted above, community marriage rates dropped off dramatically after 1810 (41.7% down to 18.2% (1811-1820). Between 1831 and 1840, the community marriage rate was 25.0%. Beginning in 1841, the rate jumped up to 45.5%. This was a clear sign of improvement on the reservation that coincided with Beach's change in management practice.

The reservation itself to a great degree became another village within the town of Kent. Through the efforts of Truman Bradley, Value Kilson and John Mauwee, the reservation became essentially an extended-family-run farm under the direction and supervision of the state overseer, Abel Beach (1844-1853).

The Schaghticoke as a community owes Abel Beach a debt of gratitude for its survival that it has never acknowledged. By turning a dependency relationship around to one of self-reliance, the reservation community survived. The fact remains that this reservation community never achieved political autonomy during this period. Based upon Beach's records, the apparent smallness of the reservation population (circa 1850: 9-10 individuals) also forestalled the development of any internal political leadership. It could not be considered an Indian tribe.

Summary

Beach's presence as the state-appointed overseer, benevolent as it may have been, contributed significantly to the lack of internal leadership development within the Schaghticoke reservation community. Beach's home was near the reservation. He was the "boss" upon whom the adult male members of the Schaghticoke reservation community depended for their livelihood. He controlled the purse strings of the reservation. He doled out assistance to individuals. He provided care when they were ill or injured. He buried their dead. As he did in the past, he could have farmed out these labors to the non-Indian population. Instead, as their overseer he engaged community members in productive labor. Beach created an early version of "workfare." He reversed the way of doing things. He created a cash economy on the reservation. By doing so, the reservation community could connect into and participate in the outside local economy. Most importantly, Beach, for the time being, broke the chains of dependency. Life within the community improved. More community members were marrying one another. Fewer were leaving.

Another unintended consequence of Beach's action was the preservation of the reservation lands. Once this cash economy took hold, the demands upon the Schaghticoke fund lessened. This decrease meant no further sales of reservation lands for this reason were needed, and none for this purpose of support occurred.

Thus, we have seen the founding and development of a community through time. The enabling conditions for its founding have been discerned. We have examined the factors that brought it into being. It was always a story of "almost, but not quite" a fully functioning community. Both its external and internal social and political environments constrained its full development. Was it ever an Indian tribe in the historical sense?[23] No. Was it a community through time? Yes. Was it self-governing? No.

What about their qualifying as a tribe under BIA guidelines? One of the Federal criteria (25 CFR 83.7 (e)) requires:

> The petitioner's membership consists of individuals who descend from a historical Indian tribe or from historical Indian tribes which combined and functioned as a single autonomous political entity.

BIA (25 CFR 83.1) defines "historical" as "dating from first sustained contact with non-Indians." Clearly on the basis of the historical evidence presented in this book, the Schaghticoke did not meet the "historical tribe" requirement. There was no Schaghticoke tribe in existence in the region at the time of sustained contact with colonial settlers. The Schaghticoke did not come into existence as a result of two historical tribes voluntarily uniting to become the Schaghticoke. There was no merging of the historic Mahican and Potatuck tribes. There was no merging of the Potatuck and Paugussett tribes that morphed into the Schaghticoke. The Schaghticoke Tribal Nation, if BIA had reviewed the historical material submitted without bias (the historian on the BIA's Schaghticoke recognition team in a memo dismissed the submitted material on the basis that she was not going to read a legal brief), would have had no choice but to have denied recognition on this criteria.

A second criteria was also important: that of continuous political authority (24 CFR 83.7 (c)), "The Petitioner has maintained political influence or authority over its members as an autonomous[24] entity." We have noted that the settlement at Schaghticoke was established in Mahican tribal territory. Schaghticoke was under the authority of a Mahican sachem (Stephen) until 1749. From 1636 until 1749, the Indians at Schaghticoke could not have been an autonomous tribe for this reason. From 1749 until the closing of the Moravian mission in 1770, the Indian settlement at Schaghticoke was schismatic in the sense that two separate Indian communities resided there. Neither controlled or had authority over the other. As we have noted, one was controlled by the Moravians with Gideon as their Indian steward. The other, non-convert community, was completely autonomous from the first. There is no evidence that this autonomous community had any defined political leadership. The two communities were politically, culturally, and ideologically different. During the post-Moravian period (1770-1790), we do find a community leadership present among the Schaghticoke. From 1800-1854 there is no evidence that such an authority was in existence. We note that the BIA criteria require a "continuous" political authority from historical times. It cannot be argued that there is a lack of historical records for this region during this period. Of all the regions in Connecticut, the historical record for this area is perhaps the most complete. The Schaghticoke Tribal Nation could not have met either the "continuous" or autonomous requirements.

Initially, the BIA tried to "fudge" the data and invent "novel" categories of evidence such as "state recognition." They were caught and forced to go back and do it again. The second time they almost got it right. But nonetheless, it was right enough.

Repass

Who were the Schaghticoke Indians? Where did they come from? Were they native to the Kent, Connecticut area? Did they represent the amalgamation of many tribal remnants or were they the continuation of a single historical tribe?

The Schaghticoke Indians appeared as a result of historical occurrences at work both far and near. Schaghticoke was the product of two cultures in collision and its consequences. Schaghticoke as a community did not pre-exist the advent of continuous historical contact with Europeans, but was created by it. This community had no one single source; it did not emerge from a single people. The origins and background of the people of Schaghticoke were legion. Schaghticoke represented a continuation not of a tribe or tribes, but of individuals' disrupted lives. Individuals who, for personal reasons we will never entirely know, sought shelter from the storm of change at "a bow in the river" at Gideon's calling.

NOTES

Introduction

[1] The Moravian Church, a Protestant denomination was organized in Bohemia (the present Czech Republic) in 1457. The Church began missionary activities in North America in 1735. The North American Church settled at, and founded Bethlehem, Pennsylvania in 1741. The Church founded three Indian missions in the area of this study, Shecomeko, Wequanach, and Pachgathgoch.

[2] Barzillai Slossom (1812, *History of Kent*, mss., 3), claims that the Schaghticoke "are the descendants of the remnant of 'Pequods' who escaped destruction" in 1637. Benjamin Trumbull (1818, *A Complete History of Connecticut, Civil and Ecclesiastical*, II:83) attributed Schaghticoke's founding to Mowehue who "invited the Indians at New Milford, from the Oblong in the province of New York, and from various other places, to settle with him at Scatacook." William Deforest (1851, *History of the Indians of Connecticut from the Earliest Known Period to 1850*, 407), believed that the Schaghticoke were "formed by the bands of wanderers who retreated before the advancing colonists." Samuel Orcutt (1882, *The Indians of the Housatonic and Naugatuck Valleys*, IV) stated that Schaghticoke was settled many hundreds of years ago by Indians from the Mahican village of Shekomeko (New York). Frederick Hodge (1910, *Handbook of American Indians North of Mexico*, pt. 2:485-486) noted that Schaghticoke was founded by a Pequot Indian by the name of Mauwehu who gathered together remnants from the Paugussett, Uncowa, and Potatuck tribes of the Housatonic River Valley at Schaghticoke around 1730. Franz Wojciechowski (1992, *Ethnohistory of the Paugussett Tribes*, 89-90) believed that the Schaghticoke were a historical continuation of his "Weantinock" tribe.

[3] Colin G. Colloway, *New Worlds for All: Indians, Europeans and the Remaking of Early America* (Baltimore: John Hopkins University Press, 1997), 3.

Chapter One

[1] John R. Broadhead, *History of the State of New York, First Period 1609-1664* (New York: Harper & Brothers, 1853), 151.

82   GIDEON'S CALLING

² ibid, 152.

³ See Francis X. Moloney, *The Fur Trade in New England 1620-1676* (Cambridge, MA: Harvard University Press, 1931).

⁴ Stephen Innes, Labor in a New Land: Economy and Society in Seventeenth-Century Springfield (Princeton, NJ: Princeton University Press, 1983), 4-5.

⁵ Alden T.Vaughan, *New England Frontier: Puritans and Indians 1620-1675* (W.W. Norton, New York, 1979), 149-150. Aiding Captain Mason at the Mystic fight were warriors from the Narragansett, Niantic, Mohegan tribes, and some disaffected Pequot. The Indians aiding the colonists in the Swamp fight battle were members of the Montauk tribe from Long Island, led by their sachem Wiandance (see Faren R. Siminoff, *Crossing the Sound: The Rise of Atlantic American Communities in Seventeenth Century Eastern Long Island* (New York: New York University Press, 2004), 63-64.

⁶ Stratford (Connecticut) Land Records, 1:243-244, *Testimony of Thomas Stanton* May 4, 1659.

⁷ Colonial Records of Connecticut, 2:339-340.

⁸ King Phillip's War (1677), King William's War, (1689), King George's War (1744), French and Indian War (1756).

⁹ Patrick Frazier, *The Mohegans of Stockbridge* (Lincoln: University of Nebraska Press, 1992), 5.

¹⁰ The English had seized the Dutch colony, which then became an English Province under the King's grant to the Duke of York. See Richard Dunn, *Puritans and Yankees: The Winthrop Dynasty of New England 1630-1747*, (1962), 148-156. Having seized the Dutch province by force, the English received the Dutch surrender at Fort Amsterdam (the present-day Battery on lower Manhattan Island, which was renamed Fort James). In the 1668 Treaty of Breda, formally ending the conflict between England and the Dutch States, the Dutch confirmed the English to be in rightful possession of New Netherland. The province was under the Duke's Patent until the advent of the Third Anglo-Dutch War (1672-1674). In August of 1673, Dutch forces seized New York from the English. Under the conditions for the cessation of hostilities stipulated in the February 1674 Treaty of Westminster, the Dutch returned possession of New York to the King of

England. The Duke's grant was reconfirmed by his brother, King Charles II.

Chapter Two

[1] Colonial Records of Connecticut, 1:28-29 (1639); Stratford Connecticut Land Records, 1:242-244; Connecticut Colonial Records, 2:339-340.

[2] Stratford Connecticut Land Records, 1:224.

[3] Colonial Records of Connecticut, 1:335-336 (1659).

[4] Talcott Papers, Correspondence and Documents, 1896, Collections of the Connecticut Historical Society, V:402.

[5] Settlers who provided the "up-front" monies for the purchase of a land grant became known as proprietors, or corporate owners of a land grant. It was to this corporate group of initial investors that a land grant and its land title were given. These new investors also had to obtain the native right or Indian title from any tribes inhabiting their granted lands, that is unless the lands had been previously obtained by the colony. Once a settlement was established it was called a plantation. These proprietors made initial land divisions amongst themselves, allotting homestead and pasturage tracts of land to each. They as a corporate group made agreements to set aside certain lands for commonage (pasturage, timber, etc. as well as water rights to rivers and streams) or common use by the proprietors. Thus these initial proprietors were also termed "commoners." Once this initial phase of settlement was completed and its associated legal, religious, and political structures put in place (townsmen [selectmen], constables, justices of the peace, fencers, pounders, listers...) the plantation became a town liable for taxation by the colony.

[6] The Paugussett at the time of first sustained contact were led by the sagamore *Ansantaway*. He also acted as sachem of the Paugussett village (*Wepawaug*) located in present-day Milford. The Paugussett village (*Cupeag*) that was located in present-day Stratford was led by Ansantaways' son *Akenach*. A third village (*Pagaset*) located at the fork of the Housatonic and Naugatuck rivers was led by Ansantaway's other son *Towtantane*.

[7] Title to these lands was ceded to the King of England by virtue of "Title by Discovery" in 1498 by John Cabot's discovery of this region while sailing under a charter issued by his sovereign. Under accepted

international law of the time such a claim could be made if the inhabitants of the newly discovered lands were not Christian, did not practice animal husbandry, or live in fixed settlements and the lands had not been previously claimed by a Christian prince. As such, the Indians retained a "natural right" or right of occupancy as tenants to the land.

[8] Colonial Records of Connecticut, 3:55 (1680).

[9] Talcott Papers, Correspondence and Documents, 1896, Collections of the Connecticut Historical Society, V:401.

[10] Colonial Records of Connecticut, 3:355 (1680).

[11] Talcott Papers, Correspondence and Documents, 1896, Collections of the Connecticut Historical Society, V:400.

[12] ibid., V:399.

[13] ibid., V:402.

Chapter Three

[1] Patrick Frazier, *The Mohicans of Stockbridge* (Lincoln: University of Nebraska Press, 1992), 46.

[2] *Journal of John Sergent 1740,* 16 (Manuscript Copy, Stockbridge, Massachusetts Library).

[3] Ted Brasser, *Riding on the Frontier's Crest: Mahican Indian Culture and Culture Change* (Ottawa: National Museum of Canada, Ethnology Division, Paper No. 13, 1974), 33.

[4] Samuel Hopkins, *Historic Memoirs of the Housatonic Indians* (Boston: S. Kneeland, 1753), 153-154.

[5] Charles J. Hoadley, ed., *Records of the Colony and Plantation of New Haven from 1638-1649* (Hartford: Case Tiffany, 1857), I:265.

[6] E. B. O'Callahan, *Documents Relative to the Colonial History of New York* (Albany: Weed Parsons, 1861), 13:345.

[7] Blair Rudes, *Resurrecting Wampano (Quiripi) from the Dead,* Anthropological Linguistics, (Bloomington: Indiana University, Department of Anthropology, 1997) Volume 39, Number 1.

[8] Lawrence H. Leder, *The Livingston Indian Records: 1666-1723* (Gettysburg: The Pennsylvania Historical Association, 1956), 108.

[9] William Cothern (1871, *History of Woodbury, Connecticut*, v.1:108) postulated a model that closely followed that depicted in the primary source data. His basic thesis was that "...the Indians of Woodbury, New Milford and Kent, have been treated as though they were one people, which is strictly correct except in regard to the Kent Indians." Cothern further noted that "The Indians residing at these two places [Potatuck and Weantinock]...have never been but two clans of the same tribe...." (ibid., 103).

[10] September 15, 1720, Meeting of the Governor and Council in New Haven, Resolve Issued, Connecticut Colonial Records, 6:203-204.

[11] New Milford Connecticut Land Records, 1:73. As we shall see, it turns out Nepato was a Mahican village sachem and the village was Weataug.

[12] Stratford Connecticut Land Records, 2:466, April 25, 1671.

[13] New Milford Connecticut Land Records, 2:3, August 29, 1705.

[14] Lawrence H. Leder, *The Livingston Indian Records: 1666-1723* (Gettysburg: The Pennsylvania Historical Association, 1956), 108-109.

[15] New Milford Connecticut Land Records, 2:3, August 29, 1705.

[16] "A List or thee Numbers & Names of the Indians belonging to, or Residing in ye County of New Haven & Fayrefield: Taken the 28th & 30th of August a d by John Minor" August 28-30, 1703, Winthrop Papers, Massachusetts Historical Society, ser. 4:150.

[17] Talcott Papers, Correspondence and Documents, Volume II 1737-41; Collections, Connecticut Historical Society, Volume V 397-398, September 30, 1725.

[18] Memorial of New Milford and Potatuck Indians to the General Assembly, Law Papers, Connecticut Historical Society, 42, May 1742.

[19] November 5, 1703, Woodbury Deed, Lands in Dutchess County, New York, cited in Shirley Dunn, *The Mohegan World 1680-1750*, Fleischmanns, NY: Purple Mountain Press, 2000), 319.

[20] Rev. Daniel Boardman, Letter, November 4, 1722, Smithsonian Institute, National Anthropological Archives Ms. 4367

[21] Gottlob & Buttners Journal, February 22,-April 9, 1742, Moravian Archives Box (B) 111, Folder (f) 2, item (i) 3b.
"...Indians came from Potatick one of which was baptized two years ago by an English minister & beg'd we would send them a teacher..."

[22] Memorial of New Milford and Potatuck Indians to the General Assembly, Law Papers, Connecticut Historical Society, 42, May 1742.

[23] Journal of Myron Mack, June 26-February 18, 1743, Moravian Archives B.111, f. 3, i. 3.

[24] Pachgatgook Mission, Moravian Archives B.111, f.2.

[25] Pachgatgoch: Bruninger, and Rundt's Diary, Moravian Archives B.115, f.3.

[26] Ezra Stiles, *Itineraries and Memoirs* 1:399, 1760, Benecke Rare Book Library, Yale University.

[27] May 17, 1758, Woodbury Burial Ground Purchase, Woodbury Connecticut Land Records, 12:120; May 16, 1758, Woodbury Potatuck Purchase, Woodbury Connecticut Land Records, 12:118; May 29, 1758, Woodbury Pootatuck Brook Purchase, Woodbury Connecticut Land Records 12:119; November 17, 1758, Woodbury Indian Land Purchase, Woodbury Connecticut Land Records, 12:118.

[28] Cherre later became a Moravian convert at Schaighticoke, assuming the name Soloman #382. He along with his wife Gertrude #392 removed to the Moravian mission at Gnadenhutten in Pennsylvania. He died there in June of 1764.

Chapter Four

[1] Resolve of the Connecticut General Assembly. (Connecticut Colonial Records 6:512)

[2] Connecticut Colonial Records 8:38

[3] Franz L. Wojciechowski, *Ethnohistory of the Paugussett Tribes: An Exercise in Research Methodology* (Amsterdam, The Netherlands: De Kiva, 1992), 81-88. Wojciechowski claims that the Weantinock were a tribe separate from the Potatuck.

[4] circa 1783, "A small party, company, or collection of persons, animals, or things" *The Shorter Oxford Dictionary on Historical Principles* II, (Cambridge: Oxford University Press, 1950 ed.).

[5] Connecticut Colonial Records 6:512. "there is discovery of Indians in the wilderness above of north of Litchfield and New Milford..."

[6] "This Assembly being informed that a parcel of Indians that sometime dwelt at New Milford are removed and settled on the west side of Ousatunnuck River, in a bow of the west side thereof, about three or four miles above New Fairfield, upon a piece of plain there, and have a desire to continue at said place"

[7] Benjamin Trumbull, *A Complete History of Connecticut, Civil and Ecclesiastical* (New Haven: Maltby, Goldsmith, 1818), 2:107.

[8] Connecticut Colonial Records 8:121-124; Town of Kent Connecticut, Land Records 12:554.

[9] Connecticut Colonial Records 7:412-413; Kent Proprietors Records I:148-149.

[10] "Whereupon it is resolved by this Assembly, that no person shall lay out any grant or farm on said plain piece of land without the special leave of this Assembly. And it is further hereby enacted and declared, that whoever shall, contrary to this order, survey or cause to be surveyed or laid out any grant of this Court in the place aforesaid, shall not hereby procure any title thereto."

[11] Connecticut Colonial Records 4:402, 1663 Order of the General Court: "...that no person in this Colony shall buy, hire, or receive as a gift any parcel of land or lands of any Indian or Indians, for the future except he does buy or receive the same for the use of the Colony or the benefit of some Town with the allowance of the court."

[12] Connecticut Archives, Indian Papers ser.1, II:75, May 1752.

[13] Connecticut Colonial Records 10:108.

[14] Moravian Archives B.111, f.3, i.3.

[15] Phillip Colee, *The Housatonic-Stockbridge Indians 1734-1749* (Albany SUNY, 1977), 94.

[16] New Milford Connecticut Land Records 1:73-75, June 19, 1716.

[17] Cited in Samuel Orcutt, *The Indians of the Housatonic and Naugatuck Valleys* (Hartford: Case, Lockwood, and Brainard, 1882), 118-119. Orcutt cites Colony Records of Deeds and Patents, vol. 3 as his source.

[18] New Milford Connecticut Land Records 2:176. August 29, 1720.

[19] Connecticut Archives, Towns and Lands, 1st series, v.7, doc 245a. January 27, 1721.

[20] Shirley Dunn, *The Mohegan World 1680-1750*, (Fleischmanns, NY: Purple Mountain Press, 2000), 322.

[21] Connecticut Archives, Towns and Lands, ser. 18, pt. 2:177 (see also Connecticut Colonial Records 9:139-140). October 8, 1743.

[22] Moravian Archives B.111, f.3, i.3; George H. Loskiel, *The History of the Mission of the United Brethren Among the Indians of North America* (London: Brethren's Society for the Furtherance of the Gospel, 1794), 68-71.

[23] Connecticut Archives, Towns and Lands, ser. 18, pt. 2:175. May 15, 1745.

[24] Moravian Archives B.111, f.2, i.3.

[25] Connecticut Archives, Towns and Lands, ser. 18, pt. 1, doc. 4. April 24, 1729.

[26] Moravian Archives B.113, f.5, i.9. October 17, 1743.

[27] George H. Loskiel, *History of the Mission of the United Brethren Among the Indians of North America* (London: Brethren's Society for the Furtherance of the Gospel, 1794), pt. 2:43.

[28] Connecticut Archives, Towns and Lands, First Series, vol. 8, pt. 1, doc 4. April 1729.

Chapter Five

[1] Patrick Frazier, *The Mohegans of Stockbridge* (Lincoln: University of Nebraska Press, 1992), 59.

[2] Matrilienal means that descent is traced exclusively through the mother's female line. Matrilocal means that a couple's residence is with the wife's lineage or clan.

[3] Ted Brasser, *Riding on the Frontier's Crest: Mahican Indian Culture and Culture Change* (Ottawa: National Museum of Canada, Ethnology Division, Paper No. 13, 1974), 28-29.

[4] Moravian Archives B.115, f.14, i.1.

[5] Moravian Archives B.115, f.114, i.1.

[6] Moravian Archives B.313, f.1, i.1.

[7] Moravian Archives B.313, f.2.

[8] Connecticut State Archives, Indian Papers, ser. 1I:244

[9] Fitch Papers 1:61-2, Connecticut Historical Society Collections.

[10] Connecticut State Archives, Indian Papers, ser.1I:244-244b.

[11] *Journal of John Sergent 1740*, 1, 5, 7 (Stockbridge, Massachusetts Library Collections).

[12] Moravian Archives B.114, f.4, i.2.

[13] Patrick Frazier, *The Mohegans of Stockbridge* (Lincoln: University of Nebraska Press, 1992), 102; George H. Loskiel, *History of the Mission of the United Brethren Among the Indians of North America* (London: Brethren's Society for the Furtherance of the Gospel, 1794), 83-85.

[14] Moravian Archives B.115, f.15.

[15] Franz L. Wojciechowski, *Ethnohistory of the Paugussett Tribes: An Exercise in Research Methodology* (Amsterdam, The Netherlands: De Kiva, 1992), 81-88.

[16] ibid., 84.

[17] Moravian Archives B.111,f.2,i.3.

[18] George H. Loskiel, *History of the Mission of the United Brethren Among the Indians of North America* (London: Brethren's Society for the Furtherance of the Gospel, 1794), pt. 2:43.

[19] Moravian Archives B.3191, f.1, Catalogue of baptized Indians in North America: #2 (Isaac), #9 (Rebecca).

[20] New Milford Connecticut Land Records 1:73-75, June 19, 1716.

[21] In: Samuel Orcutt, *The Indians of the Housatonic and Naugatuck Valleys* (Hartford: Case, Lockwood, and Brainard, 1882), 118-119. Orcutt cites Colony Records of Deeds and Patents, vol. 3 as his source.

[22] Connecticut State Archives, Towns and Lands 4:34-36.

[23] Cited in Samuel Orcutt, *The Indians of the Housatonic and Naugatuck Valleys* (Hartford: Case, Lockwood, and Brainard, 1882), 118-119. Orcutt cites Colony Records of Deeds and Patents, vol. 3 as his source.

[24] Connecticut Archives, Towns and Lands, First Series, vol. 8, pt. 1, doc. 4.

[25] Moravian Archives B.313, f.1.

[26] Connecticut Archives, Towns and Lands, ser. 1, vol. 8, pt. 2:175.

[27] Patrick Frazier, *The Mohegans of Stockbridge* (Lincoln: University of Nebraska Press, 1992), 60.

[28] Moravian Archives B.111, f.2, i.3.

[29] Allen Trelease, *Indian Affairs in Colonial New York: The Seventeenth Century* (Ithaca: Cornell University Press, 1959), 9.

[30] Connecticut Colonial Records 8:521.

[31] Moravian Archives B.111, f.2, i.3.

[32] Moravian Archives B.313, f.3, i.1.

[33] Franz L. Wojciechowski, *Ethnohistory of the Paugussett Tribes: An Exercise in Research Methodology* (Amsterdam, The Netherlands: De Kiva, 1992), 44.

Chapter Six

[1] Ted Brasser, *Riding on the Frontier's Crest: Mahican Indian Culture and Culture Change* (Ottawa: National Museum of Canada, Ethnology Division, Paper No. 13, 1974), 30-31. See also, Shirley Dunn, *The Mohegan World 1680-1750* (Fleischmanns, NY: Purple Mountain Press, 2000).

[2] See James Lynch, "The Iroquois Confederacy and the Adoption and Administration of Non-Iroquois Individuals and Groups Prior to 1756." In: Man in the Northeast, Vol. 38, Fall 1985.

³ Moravian Archives B.111, f.2, i.3.

⁴ Gideon according to the Old Testament (Judges 6-8) was one of the great Hebrew judges and military leaders of ancient Israel.

⁵ Moravian Archives B.111, f.3, i.3.

⁶ George H. Loskiel, *History of the Mission of the United Brethren Among the Indians of North America* (London: Brethren's Society for the Furtherance of the Gospel, 1794), pt. 2:44.

⁷ Moravian Archives B.115, f.15, i.20.

⁸ Moravian Archives B.115, f.4.

⁹ Moravian Archives B.111, f.3, i.3.

¹⁰ Moravian Archives B.115, f.15, i.6.

¹¹ Moravian Archives B.115, f.14.

¹² Moravian Archives B115, f.15, i.6.

¹³ Ezra Stiles, *Itineraries and Memoirs* 5:160, 1794, Benecke Rare Book Library, Yale University.

¹⁴ Moravian Archives B.115, f.12.

¹⁵ Moravian Archives B.111, f.3, i.3.

¹⁶ Moravian Archives B.111, f.2.

¹⁷ Moravian Archives B.111, f.2, i.7.

¹⁸ Moravian Archives B.313, f.1, i.8.

¹⁹ Moravian Archives B.114, f.6.

²⁰ Moravian Archives B.115, f.11.

²¹ Moravian Archives B.115, f.11.

²² Moravian Archives B.114, f.4; B.115, f.11.

²³ Moravian Archives B.114, f.6.

²⁴ Moravian Archives B.115, f.2.

²⁵ Moravian Archives B.115, f.12.

²⁶ Moravian Archives B.115, f.9.

[27] Samuel Hopkins, Historical Memoirs Relating to the Housatonic Indians (Boston: S. Kneeland, 1753), 137.

[28] Moravian Archives B.115, f.14, i.1.

[29] In 1752 the Moravians (Moravian Archives B.115, f.15, i.6) described the lands they were utilizing, "They have at present for eighteen families but a small piece which lies between the Houstonic River and Pachgatgoth Hill...Your Petrs Land begins at Rowleys Creek To which Creek a Plain or flat piece of Land runs and is continued along this beforementioned River....Your Petrs therefore humbly pray your Honors to grant them the aforementioned Plain or flatpiece of land to plant corn...." The plain at the bow of the river opposite Kent that the Moravians were requesting was those lands previously granted by the colony to Elisha Williams and is the site of present-day Kent School.

[30] Moravian Archives B.114, f.6.

[31] Moravian Archives B114, f.4.

[32] Connecticut Archives, Indian Papers, ser. 2, II:76.

[33] Tcherry (Chere) who signed this petition was not the Chere who was the sachem at Potatuck, but was, according to Moravian records his son Sam Chere or Tcherry. His father was a son of Waramaug, the Potatuck sagamore. The elder Chere's brothers were Christian and Petrus (Sherman).

[34] Connecticut Colonial Records 10:108; Connecticut Archives, Indian Papers, ser. 1, II:75.

[35] Connecticut Colonial Records 12:217-218, Connecticut Archives, Indian Papers, ser. 1, II:207.

Chapter Seven

[1] Connecticut Colonial Records 10:579.

[2] Connecticut Archives, Indian Papers ser. 1, II:77.

[3] Moravian Archives B.115, f.9.

[4] Moravian Archives B.115, f.11.

[5] Moravian Archives B.115, f.12.

[6] ibid.

[7] ibid.

[8] Moravian Archives B.115, f.9.

[9] Connecticut Colonial Records 10:34-35; Moravian Archives B.115, f.15.

[10] Moravian Archives B.115, f.9.

[11] ibid.

[12] Moravian Archives B.115, f.11.

[13] Moravian Archives B.115, f.9/f.11.

[14] Moravian Archives B.115, f.12.

[15] Moravian Archives B.115, f.11.

[16] ibid.

[17] ibid.

[18] Moravian Archives B.114, f.15.

[19] Moravian Archives B.115, f.12.

[20] ibid.

[21] Ezra Stiles, *Itineraries and Memoirs* 5:160, 1794, Benecke Rare Book Library, Yale University.

[22] Moravian Archives B115, f.10.

[23] Moravian Archives B.115, f.12.

[24] ibid.

[25] Pitkin Papers, Connecticut Historical Society Collections XIX:5.

[26] Connecticut Archives, Indian Papers, ser. 1, II: 200-200b.

Chapter Eight

[1] Connecticut Archives, Indian Papers, ser. 1, II:201.

[2] Connecticut Archives, Indian Papers, ser. 1, II:202.

[3] Connecticut Archives, Indian Papers, ser. 1, II:205.

[4] Connecticut Archives, Indian Papers, ser. 1, II:201; Connecticut Colonial Records13:542.

[5] Connecticut Colonial Records 14:196.

[6] Connecticut Archives, Indian Papers, ser. 1, II:206a.

[7] Connecticut Archives, Indian Papers. ser. 1, II:218c.

[8] Connecticut Archives, Indian Papers, ser. 2, II:50.

[9] May 6, 1783, Memorial of Abraham Fuller on behalf of the Schaighticoke asking permission to sell thirty-forty acres of reserve land. Connecticut Archives, Indian Papers, ser. 1, II:215:

"To the Honorable Generall Assembly to be Holden at Hartford on the Second Thursday of May 1783

The Memorial of Abraham Fuller of Kent in the county of Litchfield in the State of Connecticut overseer and Conservator of the Indian Natives of Scaticook in said Kent Humbly Showeth that there is a peice of Land Belonging to said Scaticook Lying ajoying the Warrups farm on the Southwardly Corner of said Scaticook Lying Contiguous to New York Line and Remote from the Improvements in said Scaticook and at present unimproved & mainly unimproveable and Lying so far out of the way of your memorialist that Great Incroachments are almost continually made upon it and the Timber almost all Cut off by people Living in the State of NewYork whereby your memorialist is under great inconvenience to Prosicute Said Trespass and that the Chief value of said Land is the Timber and your Memorialist fending of Sickness among those Natives to the Doctors and other Necesary Expense and Some old and Helpless is Humbly of opinion that It would be most Benificial to make Sale of about Thirty or Forty acres of said Land which is Rough and Rocky the Greatest Part on the Side of the Mountain and the Money arising from said Sail be put to Inntrest for the Releaf of those in Distress and want

Your Memorialist would therefore Humbly Pray your Honors to Impower your Memorialist or some other Meet Person to Make Sale of Said Land by the appraiseal of Some Meet Persons or in Some other way and Manner for the above Mentioned Purpose as Your Honors in your Great Wisdom Shall Judge Best as your Memorialist in Duty Bound Shall Ever Pray."

[10] Resolve of the Assembly, Connecticut Archives, Indian Papers, ser. 1, II:216:

> "...Resolvd by this assembly that the Sd Abraham fuller be Impowerd And is Hereby Impowerd to Sell forty Acres of the abovesd Land at the Apraizel of Indeferent men And to Execute a Deed or Deeds to the Person or persons Purchasing the Same And to Let out the Moneys Arising on thr Sale of Sd Lands on Intrest takeing good Security for the Same and the Anual Interest Arising on the Same to Be aplyd for the purpose Abovesd."

[11] Kent Connecticut Land Records 7:518.

[12] Ezra Stiles, *Itineraries and Memoirs* 5:158, 1794, Benecke Rare Book Library, Yale University.

[13] Connecticut Archives, Indian Papers, ser. 2, II:56.

[14] Connecticut Archives, Indian Papers ser. 1, 2:224.

[15] David T. Lawrence, *Eunice Mauwee, the Last of the Schaghticoke Indians*, Connecticut Historical Society, 1852, unpublished Mss.8108.

[16] Connecticut Archives, Indian Papers, ser. 2, II:56.

[17] Connecticut Archives, Indian Papers, ser. 2, II:58.

[18] Colonial Records of Connecticut 15:217, Connecticut Archives, Indian Papers, ser. 12:208.

[19] Feudalism was a political, economic, and social system that evolved in Europe and England during the Middle Ages. The term itself is derived from the Gemanic *fehu (fief, land held subject to certain conditions, an estate)* This word and concept was later borrowed by the Romans *(feudem, feodatti)*. Although the origins of this system are unclear, its development in England occurred during the post-Roman era in the aftermath of the Germanic Saxon invasions. Under Saxon rule all lands belonged to the populace (*"folcland"*, folk land). During this era the Saxon kings of England began to dole out portions of these 'folclands' to political and military allies (*vassels*). These lands in turn became known in Saxon England as *"bocland"*[19] (book land, or land given by the book) which became inheritable estates by the vassals' heirs. In turn their allegiance, homage, and service to the king were the primary requirements for the vassal's continued holding of his *fiefdom* or estate. Within these fiefdoms were manors. Manors usually consisted of several villages and constituted

the smallest economic and political unit of the system (*manorialism*). Manors were lands granted by a vassal, mostly to knights who became lesser (*mesne*) lords over the manor. The occupants of these manors were *tenants*.

[20] Manors were granted units that were in private ownership and were therefore outside both public and ecclesiastical administrative control. The mesne lord was answerable only to the vassal and the King. Legal and economic authority over the manor and its tenant occupants was vested in the lord of the manor.[20] The clergy of the manor were chosen by and owed fealty to the lord (*power of advowson*). Most tenants were bound to the mesne lord for life. At the same time such tenancy was at the sufferance of the lord of the manor. All property belonged to the lord. The tenants were required to render service to the lord by working his lands (*corvee* or *riding*) as well as those manoral lands that were *allotted* to the tenant for his use. This form of land tenure was known as *villeinage* the precursor to the form of land tenor that later became known as *commonage*. On the other hand, the lord was obliged to protect the manors tenants. In feudal England this protection was of critical importance to the tenants.

[21] 1719 *An Act for the relieving and ordering of Idiots, impotent, diftracted, and idle Perfons.*

> ...Be it further enacted, That the Selectmen...shall find any Perfon or Perfons that are reduced, or likely to be reduced to Want by idlenefs, Mifmanagement, or by bad Hufbandry, that fuch Select-man may appoint an Overseer to Advife, direct, and order fuch Person in the Management of his Bufinefs for such Time or Times as they think proper...no fuch Perfon, while under fuch appointment, fhall be able to make any Bargain or Contract, without the Confent of fuch Overseer, that shall be binding or valid under Law.

> ...And when the Select-men fhall have thus taken into their Care any fuch Perfon, and Difpofed of him as aforesaid;...the Select-men for the time being are authorized and fully empowered, by and with the advice of the said Affiftant or Justice to take into their hands and Cuftody, all the lands, Goods Chattels and Credits of any Fuch Perfon, and the fame to difpofe of, improve and manage by themselves, or any under them, for the beft Good and Advantage of fuch Perfon, of his Heirs.

Always provided, That no select-man fhall have Liberty to fell the Lands of any fuch poor, or idle perfon, without the Order of the General Assembly."

[22] Edward W. Capen, *The Historical Development of the Poor Laws in Connecticut* (New York, Columbia University Press,1905), 77

[23] ibid., 47 ff.

[24] Connecticut Colonial Records 15:217; Connecticut Archives, Indian Papers, ser. 1, II:208, December, 1775:

"Upon the Memorial of Abraham Fuller, of Kent in the county of Litchfield, shewing to this Assembly that he is overseer of the Indians at Scatacook, and that there has been considerable expense incurred curing sickness and wounds of said Indians, as per memorial on file, on which Maj. Samuel Canfield and Capt. Sherman Boardman were appointed a committee who have now made their report that the Indians have about 120 acres of land, improved and lying in one common field, that the same was formerly allotted out to each Indian, and therefore can be let out for but little profit, and that many of the said Indians are now removed and they are reduced to a small number, and that it is advisable that said lands be leased to defray the expense..."

[25] Connecticut Colonial Records 12:217.

[26] Connecticut Archives, Indian Papers ser.1II:218c.

[27] Ezra Stiles, *Itineraries and Memoirs* 5:160, 1794, Benecke Rare Book Library, Yale University.

[28] Connecticut Archives, Indian Papers, ser. 2, II:50.

[29] David T. Lawrence, *Eunice Mauwee, the Last of the Scaghticoke Indians*, 1852, Connecticut Historical Society, unpublished Mss.8108.

[30] Following the Revolutionary War during the period of Confederation, Congress was given the sole right to manage and regulate Indian Affairs. The 1782 enactment of the Articles of Confederation and Perpetual Union between the States... noted:

Art. IX. The United States in Congress assembled, shall have the sole and exclusive right and power of...regulating the trade and managing all affairs with the Indians, not members of any of the states, provided that the legislative right of any state within its own limits be not infringed or violated....

The State of Connecticut clearly had jurisdiction over the Schaghticoke community.

[31] October 1, 1772, Memorial of Daniel Morwehew Indian and others Natives of Scantecook, Connecticut Archives, Indian Papers, ser.1, II:202.

[32] It must be realized and understood that Indian reservations within Connecticut were not "tribally based" in the strict sense of that term. They were in actuality state-owned "ethnic enclaves," locations were non-resident, indigent individuals having Indian ancestry were allowed by the State to reside.

State/colony appointed overseers of these reservations acted in the same capacity as their town counterparts, the town overseer of the poor.

There were two main differences between the two.

First, the reservation overseer was answerable to the colonial/state General Assembly or later the State Superior Courts. The local overseer was in turn answerable to the town Selectmen. The local overseer dealt with known destitute town residents. The State appointed overseer was dealing with many indigent Indians, or purported Indians with whom he may not have had a personal familiarity. Thus the local or town overseer could rely with certainty that the destitute individuals referred to his care by the town justice of the peace and selectmen were in fact town residents.

The state overseer's responsibility was two-fold. The maintenance of state-owned lands and the allocation of its resources for the benefit of its occupants. The state/colony overseer had no such system of checks and balances in ascertaining the ethnic or tribal legitimacy of a claimant, especially when dealing with mixed race (black/Indian) populations. This was especially so with reservation populations that were in a constant population flux or were distant kin of reservation residents resided in other state towns or even in adjoining states. Though kin, these individuals never lived in Indian tribal or community relations, but when these individuals became ill or destitute, wherein their care and well being would default onto the local community and the community was aware that this individual was ethnically an Indian, the call would go out to the reservation overseer to come and get them on the basis of ethnic affiliation. The town then could pass the cost of this person's maintenance onto the colony or State.

Thus in 1802, the Schaghticoke reservation overseers account would note services rendered to "Gideon Sherman" from "Dover New York", or in 1811 transport "Joe" from "Jason Wings" and "Jerry" from "Warren," 1816 "Margery" in "New Milford," 1820 "Joe Peenee" in "Newtown," 1822 "Jo Tomack" in "Bridgeport," "Jerry Tomack and family" from "Norwalk" (1827) or Sarah Chickens from Pines Plains, New York (1830). Though they may have had kin relations to reservation occupants, it is apparent they were not members of a reservation or tribal community.

[33] *1776 May,* Report to the General Assembly by the Committee charged to re-allot the Schaightidcoke lands. Connecticut Archives, Indian Papers, ser. 1, II:209b:

> "To the Honbl General Assembly of the Colony of Connecticut now Sitting at Hartford we your Honors Committee appointed to make a new Alllotment of the Lands at Schattikook to and Amongst the Indians proprietors of the Same, beg leave to Report that agreable to Said directions we have made an Allotment to Each proprietor or Inhabitant of such a Quantity of Land as is Necessary for his or her Improvement & Subsistence & have had the Same Duly Measured & Bounded, an Exact Plan of the whole of said Allotments with the names of each proprietor therein Written, we have procured to be made by the surveyer and put on the Records of the Town of Kent and the Said Samul Canfield reports that he has not yet assigned David Sherman in Service according to your Honors Direction, the said David having gone away some Time since + not yet returned all which is Submitted to your Honor by your Humble Servts."

[34] Timothy Dwight, *Travels in New England and New York* II, (Cambridge: Harvard University Press, 1969), 354-355.

Chapter Nine

[1] Connecticut Archives, Indian Papers, ser. 2, II:66-66d. In comparison, the Schaghticoke community had 120 acres of land under cultivation in 1775 (1774, sixty-two residents) (Connecticut Colonial Records 15:217; Connecticut Archives, Indian Papers, ser. 1, II:208) as compared to the six acres (thirty-five residents) in 1801.

[2] Ezra Stiles, *Itineraries and Memoirs* 5:157-160, 1794, Benecke Rare Book Library, Yale University.

---

[3] May, 1800, Committee Report to the General Assembly, re: Resolve of the Scaticook Indians October 1799 (Connecticut Archives, Indian Papers, ser. 2, II:61):

> "We the subscribers having been Apointed by the Honnorable General Assembly at theire Session in October last to further examin and adjust the debts charges made against the scaticook Indions by theire present Conservator and such Physitions as have been employed by him to administer to them beg leave to report to find ... It appears that the Schatecook Land rents for about 50 Dollars a year and that the expenses for fences & necessarys Supplyed the Indions has in the Course of fourteen year exceeded the income of their Lands above the sume, which debt cannot be paid unless their Lands are sold, or some Other meanes are proved besides the rent of theire Lands all which is submitted by your Honnours humble Servts."

[4] May, 1801, Resolve of the General Assembly, Connecticut Archives, Indian Papers, ser. 2, II:67-67d:

> ...It is Resolved by this Assembly, That the Hon. Herman Swift, & John Tallmudge Esqrs be and they are hereby fully Authorized & empowered to sell, & by Deed convey to such Person or Persons as will give therefor the highest price all that part of said *reserved tract* of land lying North of a Line beginning at the Ousatonick River at the mouth of a brook which runs by the Middle Gate so called, & running thence Westward in the middle of said brook to where the said Gate doth or did stand, thence due West to the line of the State of New York and the said Herman Swift & Tom Talmudge Esqrs are hereby directed by such sale to raise so much money as will forewith discharge the said debt, and also erect *for the use* of such Indians South of said Gate six houses or wigwams, which may in the whole, be expensed not exceeding Two hundred dollars, and the expenses attending such sale & conveyance and for the residue of the purchase money of the land so sold a Term of credit may be given at the discretion of said Herman & John the same being well secured by Mortgage or otherwise, & the Interest thereof made payable half yearly, which securities shall be made & taken to the Overseer of said Indians appointed by this Assembly & his successors in this office--- And the said Overseer, and his successors, are herby directed & empowered from time to time to Loan, & place at Interest, the Money arising from such sale, as the

same may be paid to him, taking good & sufficient security therefor payable as aforesaid & secured by adequate mortgages, or by two or more sufficient sureties, inhabitants of this State And the Said Herman & John shall render their Account of such Sale, expenditures, & expenses to the Court of Common Pleas for the County of Litchfield for allowance & Settlement.

[5] Timothy Dwight, *Travels in New England and New York* II, (Cambridge: Harvard University Press, 1969), 354-355.

[6] Connecticut Archives, Indian Papers, ser. 2, II:70.

[7] Account Book of Abel Beach, 3 vols. Connecticut State Archives, 974.62 K42sc.

[8] In 1812 the Schaghticoke community numbered around forty persons. Barzillai Slossom, *History of Kent*, 1812, unpublished mss., Connecticut State Archives.

[9] May 1811, Resolve of the General Assembly in regards to the Memorial of Abel Beach. Connecticut Archives, Indian Papers ser.2, II:91. The tract authorized for sale by the General Assembly totaled twenty acres of land and was sold by Abel Beach to Ezekiel Thayr on October 8, 1811. (Kent Connecticut Land Records 12:526-527.)

[10] October 11, 2005, Summary of the Criteria and Evidence: Reconsidered Final Determination Denying Federal Acknowledgement of the Petitioner Schaghticoke Tribal Nation: 36.

[11] Connecticut Archives, Indian Papers, ser. 2, II:88. Chickens inherited 200 acres of non-reservation land from his father Chickens Warrups a Pequannock Indian, who owned the land in fee simple holding:

May, 1749, Resolve of the General Assembly in response to the Memorial of Chickens Warrups. (Connecticut Archives, Indian Papers, ser. 1, II:33) (see also Connecticut Archives, Indian Papers, ser. 1, II:25, 26, 28-32):

"Upon ye Memorial of Captn Chicken an Indian alias Sam Moohawk of Reading Parish in Fairfield County...had Surveyed & Laid out to him two hundred Acres of Land by ye appointment of this Assembly at a place called Scattecook bounded as in ye Survey thereof on record and also shewing yt ye Land aforesd Laid out to ye sd John Read Esq.r...yt he had made and executed a deed of Exchange of his aforesd hundred acres Lying in two pieces as aforesd in ye Parish of Reading to ye sd John Read Esqr & to his heirs which sd deed bears date October 11 A.D. 1748 and in Consideration thereof did receive of ye John Read Esqr a deed ... being fully Authorized thereunto of ye aforesd two hundred acres praying this Assembly yt sd deeds Executed as aforesd may be allowed of ratifyed and Confirmed and Being admitted as good evidence in ye Law for conveying and fixing ye title to ye Several pieces of Land aforesd.

Resolved by this Assembly yt ye aforesd deeds of Exchange dated as aforesd be approved of and are hereby approved of ratifyed and confirmed and allowed to be good and Sufficent evidence in Law for ye conveying and fixing ye title to ye several pieces and parcels of Land in them mentioned and described and Shall or may forever hereafter be used and improved for ye purposes aforesd to all intents and purposes as other Deeds of Land by Law are or may be."

[12] In a May 1801 resolve of the General Assembly (Connecticut Archives, Indian Papers, ser. 2, II:67-67d) permission was granted to an especially appointed committee to undertake the construction of six dwellings on the reservation. Construction of these dwellings was to be paid for out of the proceeds of reservation land sales.

[13] A Connecticut State Superior Court judgment (Connecticut State Archives, Indian Papers, ser. 2, II:15-16b) issued in 1817 illustrates this point:

...that under the Laws of this State an Indian gained no Settlement by virtue of the location of his tribe or being born in any particular Town so as to charge any such Town with his maintenance...that Charles Sherman...is to all intents and purposes a State pauper...

[14] 1836, Connecticut Historical Society, Barber Collections: Kent and New Hartford: 371.

[15] 1823-1824 Skiff & Goodsell Account Book, Kent Historical Society Collections.

[16] Daniel Morehouse Account Book, Kent Historical Society Collections.

[17] Kent Historical Society Collections, 1842-1852 Lorenzo & Morehouse Account Book, 1851 South Kent Furnace Ledger. See Appendix I.

[18] Connecticut State Archives, 974.62 K42sc.

[19] According to Beach's records Joseph Mauwee apparently left the reservation in 1845. He was still in the area and was prospering sufficiently enough to open a line of credit at South Kent Furnace in 1851. Jacob Mauwee died in 1848.

[20] Lorenzo & Morehouse Account Books, Kent Historical Society Collections.

[21] Kent Furnace Co. Account Book, Kent Historical Society Collections.

[22] Asa Slade Account Book, Kent Historical Society Collections.

[23] At no point in time would this community have qualified for a federal relationship or recognition as understood by the United States Government. The *Samuel Veazie and Levi Young v. Wyman B. S. Moor*, 55 US. 568 (1852) Supreme Court decision clearly addressed the issue of Indian groups not deserving such a relationship:

> ...the Constitution manifestly refers only to independent tribes with which the general government may come in conflict; not to those small remnants of tribes scattered over the country, which are under state jurisdiction and guardianship.

[24] Under BIA regulations (25 CFR 83.1) "Autonomous" is defined as: "the exercise of political influence or authority independent of the control of any other Indian governing entity..." BIA does not recognize the jurisdiction or political control of a tribe by a state for recognition purposes. Only other Indian tribes are considered.

Appendix A

Potatuck and Schaghticoke Deeds,
Petitions and Memorials in Chronological Order

Year, Date
Location
Signatories

1668, 16 August
NW Derby, South of Four Mile River
*Atterosse, Nanatoush, Kehore Rourkowhough, _Poquonat_, _Chesusumock_
   Machetnumledge

1670, 18 May
NW Derby, Four Mile Brook (DTR.1901 308-309)
*_Coshoshemake_, Wataquenock, Wasawas, Atrechananaset Johns, Sasosoe,
   Chubbs, Keke Sunun,

1671, 25 April
Weantinock (New Milford) area, Henry Tomlinson Purchase (SLR.2: 466
   MSS.), Land 3 miles downriver from Goodyears Island and four miles
   upriver on both sides, three miles in breath from each bank. 26,000
   acres
*_Pocono_, Ringo, Quoconoco, Oromanhed, *_Cohasahamoke_
   *_Wookpeenees_, Woconoys Matazot, Tomo, Yohensats, Toto,
   Chofemheheam, Oshoron, _Papiscomos_, Pomantock,

1671, 1 July
Land South of Tomlinson Purchase, West: Housatonic River, South,
   Qunnupoge Pond (SLR.1:492 MSS.)
Peraonos, _Cakapetous_, Pockowimp, *_Caushamoke_, Quaronunqui,
   Weccompis, Apethis,

1672, 22 April
Samuel Sherman Grant, One square mile purchase. (SLR.1:384 MSS.)
*_Maquash_, Quiomp, Okenach, Instockumm, Wapsuamumm, Chakins,

1673, 26 April
Woodbury, First Purchase. Pomperaug Purchase. Conveyance was
   executed in Stratford. (WLR.2:137)
No signatories available. Copy is lost. _Yohcomge_ was one possible
   signatory as mentioned in the 14 July 1673 deed below.

1673, 5 June
Island purchase near the mouth Four Mile river, against Indian fort near
    Alexander Bryans field
*_Cushamack_, Ponomskut, Robin Pawanet, Amonequon, _Chawbrook_
    Kehow.

1673, 14 July
Woodbury, lands west and south of the Pomperaug Purchase including the
    village of Potatuck (WLR.2:136).
*_Avomockomge_, Kenonge, _Wecuppemee_.

1679, 16 April
Second Kettletown Purchase including Quaker Farms east of Eight Mile
    Brook (WLR.2:1)
Cheabrooke, "together with the consent and approbation of
    Coshusheougemy (Sachem,) the sagamore of puttatuck."

1682, 10 July
Lands west and south of the First (Pomperaug) Purchase, 1673 (WLR.2:1)
Wesuncks, Wonokekunkbom.

1685, 17 March
Shepaug or Second Purchase (WLR.2:136)
Waramaukeag, Womoqui, _Keshooshmaug_, _Chuhabaux, Youngamoush_,
    Nuccaddamo, _Papenau_ Nemoumbam, _Poquanow._

1686, 24 January
Albany meeting between the New York authorities, the Taconic and the
    Potatucks at Weantinock specifically mention that they are related to
    the Indians down river of them (Potatuck village). Leder 1956:108-9
Wanamanheet Pinawee, Pachkanass.

1687, 6 August
Derby, Quaker Farms, Rock House Hill (DTR.1901:428-430)
Cockapatony (tackamore), Nanoques, Meshiling, _Chebrooke,_ Stastockham,
    Wanxacun, _Sunkaquene_, Wetupaco, Pusseckes, _Nanawag_.

1687, 30 October
Third (Quassapaug) Purchase. (WLR.2:137)
Chevoramauge, *_Kesoshamaug_ (sagamore), Punhone, Nunawauk
    Youngstockum, Chohees, Wonokequambomb, Tantamohoh.

1698, 15 August
Weescantook Purchase. Land between 4 Mile Brook (south) 5 Mile Brook
    (north), (west) river (east) Woodbury Road. In vicinity of Rockhouse
    Hill. (DTR.1901:319-320)

*Cockapatouch, Neighbor Rutt, *Nonawauk*, Gyouson, *Mawquash*, *Cheshconeeg*, Keyxon, Raretoun, Rash-Koinoot, Tazchun, Thomasseet.

1701, 16 May
Woodbury, east side, Waterbury line, 6 square miles, (WLR.v.2:137)
Wombummaus, Nucqutosmaug, *Mashaquas*, *Cacapattanees* john Cacapattaneeg, Zmbouge "All Potatuck Indians" Jon Banks, Momanchenay *Squawneag*, *Nunnawake* Wattnuntcome.

1701, 3 September
Woodbury Deed (WLR.v.2:145)
Mauquash, Mausombaw

1702, 9 August
Confirmatory Deed of the 23 April 1671 purchase of lands adjacent to Goodyears Island. (SLR.MSS.2:497)
*Papeppto (Sachem of Oantenock) (Poconos son?), *Pocono*, *Nanhotuho*, Cush, Siecus, Metack, Matteecus.

1702, 8 February
New Milford Proprietary Deed. Bridgewater and most of New Milford (excepting Indian Field) Northernmost boundary Gaylordsville
*Papetoppe, Shoopack, Bapisc--otoo, Wewinapuc, Towwe- -comis, *Pocanus*, Wompotoo, Paramethe, *Nanhootoo*, Wewina puck, Hawwasues, *Chasqueneag*. *Yoncomis*, Papiream, Tomoseete, *Nonawak*. *Papetoppe (Pominskeed)

1705, 25 July
Newtown Proprietary Deed. Six by eight mile tract of present day Newtown. Boundaries reaffirmed in 1712 by an appointed committee. (Towns&Lands, Se.1,v.3:63-64) (NTR.1-2:15), (NLR.2:128), (NTR.1-2:48)
*Mauquash, *Massumpus*, *Nunnawauk*, Watchunaman, Waowatous, Martezuck, Awashkerum, Annumetae, Mattoucksqua,Gonnehampiska, Womperowask, Munapask, PunnantaWannomo, Mesuncksco Taroask, Merdmmoe, *Sukanunque*, Sussoujo.

1705, 29 August
New Milford, Indian Field conveyance. (ref.8 Feb.1702 New Milford deed.) (NMLR.2:3)
Shamenunckqus (alias Bapistoo) *Chesquaneag*, Whemut, Papetopo Wannupe, Cuttouckes, Mantooes Papetapos squaw, Youngams-squaw, Joman, Appacoco, *Poquanow*, Yongans.

1705, 25 October
Woodbury, third Kettletown purchase. (WLR.2:137)
Tomseet, Chyiondge, *Cotsure Wampumbom*, *Cockapatouch*

1705, 29 December
New Milford Deed (recorded in Fairfield, FLR.2:331) (referred to as the
    Mitchell Purchase)
Matchise Wanhump, *Chesquaneg*.

1706, 28 May
Woobury Confirmatory Deed (WLR.3:138)
Nunnawauk, *Tumaseet*, *Cheaquneag*, *Mauqush*, Wussebucome, Accommy,
    Wirasquancot, *Kehore*, *Wussockanunckqueen* Noegosh- emy,
    Munmenepoosqua, Muttan-umace (squa).

1710, 23 June
Woodbury, North Purchase (WLR.2:179). East- Waterbury, West- New
    Milford, South- original Woodbury bounds, Northerly-present Potatuck
    lands. Encompassed present day Bethlehem and Judea
Nunawague, *Chesquneage*, *Cockshury*, *Wussuttanunekqut*. *Mauquach*

1715, 2 March
Litchfield deed (Woodruff 185:13) northernmost Potatuck conveyance
Chusqunnoag, *Corkscrew*, *Quiump*, *Magnach*, *Kehow* Sepunkum, Poni,
    Wonposet, *Suckqunnockqueen*, *Taweeume*, *Mansumpanish*,
    Weroamaug, Wognacug, *Tonhocks*.

1716, 19 June
Benjamin Fairweather Deed north of New Milford, east side of Housatonic
    river north for 30 miles. Nepatoe resides at Kunck pacooke (located at
    or just above Kent.) The deeds text makes mention that Weramaug is a
    Kinsman to Nepatoe. (NMLR.1:73,CT.Towns and Lands IV:36-37.)
Weramaug, *Nepatoe*, *Jacob*, *Tanhook*, *Mauhehu*, *Simon*, Mantooes.
    "Indian proprietors of the land that Lies along Stratford Great River
    north from New Milford.

1720, 22 October
Waraumaug Deed East side of Housatonic river from New Milford north
    almost to the MA Border. Warren, Cornwall, Cannan, Norfolk, Goshen.
    (Colony Records of Deeds and Patents 3) (Orcutt 1882a:118-119)
Weromaug, Weraroquoin (alias-Curlow), *Nepatoo*, Ahanyeam, *Mawehew*,
    Owound, *Tawhook*, Paconopeet, Tackahound (alias-John Wawnowgh),
    Wassomaug.

1722, 23 June
Conveyance of Waramaugs Reserve excepting NW Washington and
Warren. (his son Chere sold most of the remainder in the late 1740's)
(CT. Towns and Lands IV:34-36) (KLR.I:464) (Boardman 1822
mentions that Chere and the tribe's remnants moved to Schaghticoke in
1736)
Warromaug, *Jacob*, *Shehow*, *Symon* Borredge. ("Warramaug Sachem of
Weantenuck).

1723, 7 August
Newtown Deed. All of Newtown excepting the six acres of Cockshures
field. (see NLR file for ref.) Deed for the sale of Cockshures field
(1730) is in (NLR.3-4:3-4)
Quiomph Mauchoro,Wahuncop,Machocomp, *Mausumpus*.

1728, 6 March
Woodbury (Warner) Deed SW corner west of Shepaug falls (Promiseck) of
Woodbury (Cothren 1871:31, also see WLR Ref. in Woodbury file)
Mauquash, *Cockshure*, *Conkararum*, *Chob*, *John Chob* Passacoran.

1729, 24 April
New Fairfield (Sherman) Deed. (Towns and Lands ser.1,8,pt.1 doc.4)
Cockkenon, *Mawwehue*, Catorukese, *Wonpound*, *Jacob-Curkey*, Shonin,
Quepy, *ComCuk- eson*, Ceape, Siecuss, *Jomes*, Oceres

1733, 18 January
Woodbury Deed (South Purchase I) (WLR.4:212) "Potatuck Indians in ye
Town of Woodbury"
Quiump, *Cockshure*, Manchooro, Hancuttora.

1733, 18 June
Woodbury Deed (South Purchase II) (excepting their village) (Cothren
1871:31, see also WLR.4:212) "Indian proprietors belonging to
Potatuck..."
Quiump, *Cockshure* Maucheere *Chob*, *John Chob* , Passacoran.
Nancuttora.

1733, 31 July
New Milford (SE Bridgewater) Deed. "the Intervale" or "Hawley's Plain"
400 acres near Southville on the Woodbury line at Shepaug Neck.
(NMLR.4:509)
Cockshure, "Indian of an Indian plantation within the township of
Woodbury [Potatuckvillage]" "...a certain tract parcel of land within
the township of New-Milford..."

1736, May

Resolve of the General Assembly establishing a reserve at Schaghticoke (CPR.8:38-39)

"Indians that sometime dwelt at New Milford are removed and settled on the west side of the Ousatunnuck River, in a bow on the west side thereof, about three or four miles above New Fairfield, upon a piece of plain land there..."

1741, 17, July

Kent (John Reed) Purchase 200 acres having been granted to Reed by the General Court in October 1710 and laid out by the county surveyor on 21 May 1741.(IP.ser.1,II:31)

Maweho, *Tom Cuckson James*, Watau,Coness

1742, 13 May

Petition to the General Assembly "Memorial of New Milford and Potatuck Indians to the General Assembly" (Law Papers CHS.Coll.XI:42-43)

Mowchu, *John Cockune, Job*, Pukin, *Peenes*, *Sam Cheery*, John Sherman, *Simon (Jame...)* John Hatchet. Cong

1746, 19 December

Kent, Watson & Stephens lease. (KLR.I:381)

"*Captn Mayhew*, *Leftenant –Samuel Coksurer*, *Jobe Mayhew*, John Anteney, *Thomas Cuksuer*, *John sokenoge*.

1752, May

Petition to the General Assembly"...of sundry Indians inhabitants of Pachgatgoth or Scatticook near Kent..." (IP.ser.1,II:7)

Gideon-(Mauwee) *Joshua* (Chob), (Jobe) (Job) Samuel (Jacob Curkey), (Kiop) Martins *Simons* (James) Jeremias Petrus *Gottlob* (Wapumbom) Christian Lucas Gottlieb Isaaous *Tcherry* (Cheery), (Quepy) Amos Moses

1756, 10 October

Petition to the General Assembly (IP. Ser.1, II:77)

Joshua Mauchud, Gottlieb Sockonok, Jeremia Coksure

1758, 17 May

Woodbury (Burial Ground) Purchase (WLR.12:120)

Tom Sherman, *Jeremiah Cockshure, Samuel Cockshure, Gideom Mawehu*

1758, 16 May

Woodbury (Potatuck) Purchase (WLR.12:118)

Tom Sherman, *Jeremiah Cockshure, Samuel Cockshure, Gideon Mawehu*

1758, 24 May
Woodbury (Potatuck Brook) Purchase (WLR.12:119)
Tom Sherman

1758, 17 November
Woodbury (River) Purchase (WLR.12:119)
Tom Sherman

1759, 21 May
Woodbury (Potatuck Village) Purchase (WLR.12:119)
Tom Sherman

* indicates principal signatory.

(DTR) Derby Town Records

(FLR) Fairfield Land Records

(IP) Indian Papers, Connecticut State Archives, Hartford

(KLR) Kent Land Records

(NLR) Newtown Land Records

(NMLR) New Milford Land Records)

(SLR) Stratford Land Records

(WLR) Woodbury Land Records)

Appendix B

Pachgatgoch Mission Roster

1751

Compiled from B.115, F14 Item 1.

Cross-correlated with B. 3191, F.1 / F.1a.

Name	Place/Date Baptism	Listed Affiliation
1. Gideon #33 (Mauweseman, Ammavasamon, Mauwee)	Pachgatgoch/1743	Womp.
2. Joshua #34 (Job) (son of Gideon)	Pachgatgoch/1743	Potatik/ Womp.
3. Martin #156 (Wanawahek) (son of Gideon)	Wequanach/1749	Potatik/ Womp.
4. Simon #42 (James) (son of Zacharus #19)	Shekomeko/1743	Potatik/ Womp.
5. Gottlieb #149 (Nasskaschak, Sockonok) (1756 Kent Petition to the General Assembly)	Pachgatgosh/1749	Potatik/ Womp.
6. Samuel #35 (Kiop, (Potatuck 1722-1752)	Pachgatgoch/1743	Potatik/ Womp.
7. Jeremias #40 (Jeremiah) (son of Rachel #154)	Shecomeko/1743	Potatik/ Womp.
8. Christian #166 (Pentawam) (brother of Petrus (Sherman) #165 of Potatik) and Tcherry (later #282)	Wequanach/1749	Potatik/ Womp.
9. Gottlob #161 (Wawapam, Won pound [1729], Wampumbom [1705])	Wequanach/1749	Potatik/ Womp.
10. David #198 (son of Andrew of Potatik #58)	Wequanach/1749	Potatik/ Womp.
11. Paulus #162 (Wanspachek) (son of Simon #42 & Hannah #43)	Wequanach/1749	Potatik/ Womp.
12. Johannes #254 (John, Penni, Peenees [1742]) (son of Simon #42 & Hannah #43)	Pachgatgoch/1750	Potatik/ Womp

13. Petrus #165   Wequanach/1749   Potatik/Womp.
(Nanakumawocha, Peter, Sherman) (father Warramaug Sachem of
Weantnuck, mother Maria #153, Apatanomi)

(brothers Tchsherry #282 & Christian #166)

14. Lucas #39   Shecomeko/1743   Womp.
(Quawatchonit) (died 1757 Bethlehem)

15. Amos #36   Pachgatgoch/1743   Womp.
(Buicke)

16. Jonathan #320   Pachgatgoch/1751   Potatk/ Womp.
(Maramob) (son of Martha #64 & Gideon #33 of Potatik)

17. Philippus #319   Pachgatgoch/1751   Potatik/ Womp.
(Nakpan, Philip) (son of Gottlieb #149 [Sockonok][Nasskaschak])

18. Martha #64   Wequanach/1744   Potatik/ Womp.
(second wife of Gideon#33) (daughter of Erdmuth #151 of Potatik)

19. Elisabeth #41   Shekomeko/1743   Potatik/Womp
(wife of Josua #34 (Job) son of Gideon #33) (daughter of Petrus 165 &
Thamar)

20. Magdalena #150   Pachgatgoch/1749   Mahik
(wife of Gottlieb #149 [Sockonok])

21. Justina #157   Wequanach/1749   Womp.
(Quachschawap) (wife of Martin #156 son of Gideon #33)

22. Thamar #50   Shecomeko/1743   Womp.
(wife of Petrus (Sherman) #165) (daughter Elisabeth #41 married to Josua
#34 son of Gideon #33)

23. Agnes #195   Wequanach/1745   Potatik/ Womp.
(daughter of Petrus #165 & Thamar #50)

24. Lucia #155   Pachgatgoch/1749   Womp.
(Nooskaelekan) (wife of Samuel #35 of Potatik)

25. Gottlieba #197   Wequanach/1749   Potatik/ Womp.
(Quich) (daughter of Sara #230 of Potatik sister of Gottlieb #149) (married
to Kehore, later Abraham)

26. Juliana #196   Wequanach/1749   Potatik/ Womp.
(daughter of Gideon #33 & Martha #64) (wife of Gottlob #161)

27. Rebecca #280   Pachgatgoch/1750   Potatik/Womp.
(Wanumpeki) (wife of David # 304 [Warrups], Grandaughter of Maria
#153 mother of Tchsherry-later Solomon #382 brother of Petrus #165)

28. Lea #67   Shecomeko/1744   Potatik/ Womp.
(second wife of Gideon #33) (former wife of Andrew #53 John Anthony of
Potatik)(died 3/23/49)

29. Sara #252   Pachgatgoch/1750   Potatik/ Womp.
(daughter of Sara #230 of Potatik, sister of Gottliebe #1970) (married to
Kehore later Abraham #381)

30. Charitas #159   Wequanach/1749   Potatik/ Womp.
(Kiwaasetaschquah) (daughter of Petrus #165 & Thamar #50) (wife of
Abel #63, a Hooglander)

31. Priscilla #56   Shecomeko/1747   Womp.
(wife of Simeon #42 [former James]), (previously married to Lucas #39
who died at Bethlehem 1747)

32. Erdmuth #151   Pachgatgoch/1749   Potatik/Womp.
(Tschanatamsquah) (mother of Martha #64 of Potatik) (aged 70 in 1755)

33. Maria #37   Pachgatgoch/1743   Potatik/Womp.
(married to Samuel #35 of Potatik) (daughter of Gideon #33 of Potatik)

34. Johanna #158   Wequanach/1749   Potatik/Womp.
(Meschanschquah) (daughter of Gideon #33 of Potatik)

35. Salome #231   Pachgatgoch/1749   Potatik/Womp.
(daughter of Priscilla #56 & Lucas#39)

36. Benigna #232   Pachgatgoch/1749   Potatik/Womp
(daughter of Simeon #42 [former James of Potatik] & Priscilla #56)

37. Anna #233   Pachgatgoch/1749   Potatik/Womp.
(daughter of Petrus [Sherman] #165)

38. Benigna #163   Wequanach/1749   Potatik/Womp.
(Wutakem) (daughter of Simeon #42)

39. Maria #253   Pachgatgoch/1750   Potatik/Womp.
(daughter of Kehore [later Abraham #381] & Sara #252 both of Potatik)

40. Gabriel #160   Wequanach/1749   Hooglander
(daughter of Caritas #159 [daughter of Petrus #165] & Abel #63 a
Hooglander of Shekomeko)

41. Beata #272   Pachgatgoch/1750   Potatik/Womp
(daughter of Jeremias #40 of Potatik & Agnes #195 daughter of Petrus
#165)

42. Christina #281   Pachgatgoch/1750   Potatik/Womp.
(daughter of Samuel #31 of Potatik & Lucia #155)

43. Anna #300   Pachgatgoch/1751   Potatik/Womp.
(infant daughter of Josua #34 [son of Gideon #33] & Elisabeth #41)

44. Johannes #305   Pachgatgoch/ 1751   Potatik/Womp
(John [son of Gottlieb (Sokonok)] #149 &Magdelana #150)

45. Joseph #306   Pachgatgoch/1751   Potatik/Womp
(infant son of John #254 [Peenees of Potatik] & Lea #255)

46. Jacob #317   Pachgatgoch/1751   Potatik/Womp.
(infant son of Martin #156 [son of Gideon #33] & Justina #157)

47. Lazara #60   Shecomeko/1743   Womp.

48. Cherry   not baptised   Potatik/Womp
(Tchsherry) (later Solomon #382), (father Warramaug sachem of
Weantinock, mother Maria #153 (Apatanomi) (brothers Petrus (Sherman)
#165 & Christian #166)

49. Kehore   not baptised   Potatik/Womp.
(later Abraham #381) (Kehow, Shehow, Kehor, Keehorn, Kior, Kihor)

Summary of B.115, f.14, item 1.
Of the 49 Indians listed in this roster as residing at Schaghticoke in 1751:
    46 were classed as Wompanach (Womp.).
    1 was classed as Mahican (Mahik).
    1 was classed as a Hooglander.
Of the 46 Indians residing at Schaghticoke classified as Wompanch by the
Moravians:
    39 are confirmed as being Potatuck (Potatik).
    8 remaining Wompanach on the roster have not been conclusively
    identified as Potatik.

Appendix C

August 28-30, 1703, A List of thee Numbers & Names of the Indians belonging to, or Residing in ye County of New Haven & Fayrefield: Taken the 28th & 30th of August a d by John Minor
Winthrop Papers, Massachusetts Historical Society, series 4:150.

Potatuck Indians	Oweantanuck [Weantinock] Indians
Tummasett	Pomkinset
Nunnawoake	Paecannaz
Wahmasunkoo	Chuhabaux
Youhyouwhy	Younggams
Chesquananeag	Apperock
Mawquash	Dowhooks
Wawequi	Wunnuppe
Nebowwah	Mannetoos
Towwegameags	Young Pomkinseet
Naquttunggi	Wuttoggescet
Towheag	Whemutt
Wussebunkcommun	Promises
Wusuggunnuck queen	Cocumboss
Maonnuppowrott	Chanooss
Airochuwasssuck	Petawuppe
Cokesooraw	Chebamee
Cockepaddawsh	Qunkquttanatt
Appoonee	Cowepay
Att-----h	Toummas

Appendix D

Dates of Residency of Potatuck/Wompanach listed in B.115, f.14, i.1 at Shecomeko, Wequanach, and Pachgatgoch prior to 1751.

A. Shecomeko

Name	Year
1. Simon #42	1743
2. Jeremias #40	1743
3. Lucas #39	1743
4. Elisabeth #41	1743
5. Thamar #50	1743
6. Lea #67	1743
7. Pricilla #56	1743
8. Andrew #53	1743

(Potatik/ Womp. not listed on 1751 roster.)
Total of 7 individuals who were listed on the 1751 roster.

B. Wequanach

Name	Year
1. Martin #156	1749
2. Christian #166	1749
3. Gottlob #161	1749
4. David #198	1749
5. Paulus #162	1749
6. Petrus # 165	1749
7. Martha #64 (Gideon's 2nd wife)	1744
8. Justina #157	1749
9. Agnes #195 (daughter of Petrus & Thamar)	1749
10. Gottlieba #197	1749
11. Julianna #196	1749
12. Caritas #159	1749
13. Johanna #158 (Gideon's daughter)	1749
14. Benigna # 163	1749

Summary:
12 of the 14 names cited above who were residing at Wequanach in 1749 were listed as residing at Pachgatchgoch in 1751.

With the exception of an Anna #51 there were no Wompanach residing at Wequanach prior to 1747.

All were Mahican (Mahik).

7 Wompanach came from Shecomeko to the Schaghticoke community circa. 1751.

14 Wompanach came from Wequanach to the Schaghticoke community circa.1751.

21 total from both communities to Schaghticoke.

15 of the total can be positively identified as Potatik.

Appendix E

Potatik/Wompanach in Residence at:
A. Pachgatgoch circa 1743
B. Pachgatgoch circa 1749/1750

Name	Date	Nationality
A.		
1. Gideon #33	1743	Mahican/Womp.
2. Joshua #34 (son of Gideon)	1743	Potatik/Womp.
3. Samuel #35 (married to Maria)	1743	Potatik/Womp.
4. Amos #36 1743 Womp.		
5. Maria #37 (daughter of Gideon) (married to Samuel #35)	1743	Potatik/Womp.
6. Lazara # 60 (first wife of Gideon) (died 1743 at Pachgatchgoch)	1743	Womp.
B.		
1. Gottlieb #149	1749	Potatik/Womp.
2. Magdalena # 150 (wife of Gottlieb)	1749	Mahik
3. Lucia #155 (2nd wife of Samuel #35)	1749	Womp.
4. Rebecca #280 (mother of Tscherry& Petrus)	1750	Potatik/Womp.
5. Sara #252(married to Kehore)	1750	Potatik/Womp.
6. Erdmuth #151 (mother of Gideon's 2nd wife)	1749	Potatik/Womp.
7. Salome #231	1749	Potatik/Womp.
8. Benigia #232	1749	Potatik/Womp.
9. Anna #233 (daughter of Petrus) (granddaughter of Rebecca)	1749	Potatik/Womp.
10. Maria #253 (daughter of Kehore & Sara)	1750	Potatik/Womp.
11. Beata #272	1750	Potatik/Womp.
12. Christina #281 (daughter of Samuel & Lucia)	1750	Potatik/Womp.
13. Johannes (John) #254	1750	Potatik/Womp.

Summary

Of the 13 individuals noted above, 12 were classified as Wompananch. Of these 12 Wompanach 11 were identifiable as Potatuck (Potatik).

In May of 1742 Gideon (Mauwee) described himself as one of 70 Potatuck inhabitants residing at Potatuck (Southbury) and New Milford along with Tcherry, Simon Job, Peenees (Johannes), Chob (Job) (Josua) and Sherman (Petrus).

In 1743 there were at Schaghticoke a total of 6 individuals, mostly Gideon Mauwee's extended family.

All were Wompanach, four of whom were conclusively Potatuck.

During 1743 an additional eight individuals joined the Schaghticoke community from Shecomeko. All these individuals were classified as Wompanach of whom 5 can posivtivly be identified as Potatuck.

Between 1749 and 1751, 14 more Wompanach joined Schaghticoke. Of these fourteen 12 were positively identified as Potatuck.

Also during the 1749/1750 period another 13 individuals joined the community who did not come from either Wequanach or Shecommeko. All of these individuals were identifiable Potatuck except Magdelena #150 the wife of Gottlieb (Sokonok) #149.

An additional 6 Potatuck individuals were baptised at the Pachgatchgoch mission in 1751.

Appendix F

Christian and non-Christian Indians from Schaghticoke
who Served in the French and Indian War
(derived in part from Schaghticoke Tribal Nation petition for federal
acknowledgement, v.22, doc.159)

Moravian Converts.

1. Christian (166)	1755-1757	(Pentawam, brother of Petrus Sherman)
2. Johannes (254)	1755-1757	(Penni, Peenees, son of Simon)
3. Jonathan (320)	1756-1760	(Maramob, son of Gideon Mauwee)
4. Lucas (152)	1756-1760	(may not have been from the Pachgatgosh mission)
5. Martin (156)	1759	(Wanawahek,son of Gideon Mauwee)
6. Paulus (162)	1756-1760	(Wanspachek, son of Simon)
7. Phillipus (319)	1756-1760	(Nakpan, son of Gottlieb Sokonok)
8. Samuel (35)	1757	(Kiop)
9. Johannes (305)	1759-1760	(son of Gottlieb Sokonok)
10. Gottlob (161)	1756	(Wawapom)

Non-Moravian Indians.
1. Gomop
2. Paschqua
3. Kahaijo
4. Martin
5. Joseph Cocksure
6. Stephen
7. Kihor (son)
8. David Warrup
9. Thomseed
10. Nathanel
11. Samuel Cocksure
12. Jonathan Cocksure

According to the Schaghticoke Petitioner, 158 Schaghticoke served in the French and Indian War. This claim is not supported by a documentary citation. If true, there were at least 148 adult members in the non-Moravian Indian community during this period.

Appendix G

Schaghticoke Population in 1786

At a meeting held by the Indians in Scatecook in Kent April the 13th AD 1786

We are as I would inform that the Poore Natives that are in this sd Scatecock seem to Bee kept in or undeare such Cloud of Darkness that they are not capable of acting for them sealfs Neither can they act for them sealfs Neither can they act for them sealfs by reason of their Want of education wheare fore I my sealf bee one of this tribe a Native...

Joseph Mawwee
Elihu Mawwee
Peter Mawwee
Daniel Sucknuck
John Peters
Peter Shirman
Jonas Cocksure

The Natives in Scattecook Number
the Mailes   36
the females   35
there is twenty of them school children....

Appendix H

Schaghticoke Community, 1789-1856

Ezra Stiles: Inteineries 1789
Dwight's Travels 182
Cornwall Connecticut Land Record
The Schaghticoke Overseers Account Book of Abel Beach
The Public Records of Connecticut
Litchfield County Court Records
Connecticut State Archives Indian Papers
Connecticut Special Acts &Laws

"Scatticook Tribe 1789"
From Ezra Stiles: *Inteineries*, vol. 5: 157-160

"Oct. 5 visited the Ind at Scatacook about 7 or 8 family belonging there, of wch 3 or 4 only present…"

AGE NAME

MEN

26	Levi Suckkonok
63	Saml. Cockshure
30	Peter Maw-we-hu King
16	David Sherman single
50	Peter Sherman
27	Danl. Sukkenok
50	Thos. Wallops
50	Jonas Tomuck
50	Jonas Cockshure
35	Elihu Chuse fr. Chush
70	Juno Pect
40	Jo Pene
	(12)

BOYS

15	Job Suckenok
15	Steph. Syakus
12	Dennis Mau-we-yew son of Peter Maw-we-hu
10	Joseph Mau-we-yew " " "
9	Jno Mau-we-yew " " "
8	Boy Mau-we-yew " " "
8	Isaac Skenk
6	Martin Sukernuck
3	Boy Sukernuck
3	Jer Cockshure
18	Isaac Cockshure
16	Jonas Cockshure
13	Gideon Skenk
12	Abraham Rice
10	Jer Tomuck
10	Wm. Kehore
12	Danl. Skenk
11	Abel Hinds
	(18)

SQUAWS

64	Old Su	w Juno Pect
65	Abrigail	widow
70	Joannna	w. J sau
50	Mymy	widow Suknux
19	? Lydia	
30	Molly	widow Suk
68	Sarah Chuse	wife of Chush
35	Anna	old maid
28	Eunice Sukernux	wife
25	Abrigail	wife
30	Sarah Suckernux	
45	Old Mary Suckenux	widow
25	Young Sue	widow of Tomuck
30	Sarah	wife of Elihu Chuse
40	Sibble	wife of Sherman
35	Sarah	wife of Wallops
25	Eliza	wife of Peny
28	Martha	has children
27	Eliz	wife of Pet Mauwehu Queen
30	Eunice Wallops	m. Neg
	(20)	

GIRLS

3	Roxana	Elihu's child
3	Charlotte	
4	Sally	Daugther Levi Suck
2	Laura	" " "
6	Betty Suknox	
12	Tamer Mauwehu	
12	Joana Suknux	
7	Lydia Toto	
17	Hulda Kee-hore	
19	Hanna Sherman	at New Milford
18	Phebe Hynd	
	(11)	

AD 1789 Tot 67 souls
1745 600 or 161 men
1765 102 102 counted by Assoc. Litchfield Co.
only four families on spot 1789

1798 Dwight, Timothy: *Travels in New England and New York*: **354-355**
"...From this spot the road passes through the Scaticook settlement formed by the remains of an Indian tribe of that name. The tract which they occupy is a handsome interval about three miles in length on the western border of the Housatonic. On the west it is bounded by the base of a lofty mountain. The land, naturally excellent, is miseraby cultivated, both by the Indians and their tenants...the wigwams, sixteen in number, by the degraded appearance of their woman and children..."

The editor of his notes, Barbra Miller (1969) mistakenly identified this location (footnote 11, page 411) with that of Schaghticoke New York which was established as she noted in 1676 by then Governor Andros of New York.

1799 Indian Papers ser.2,v.II :56 Petition of Peter and Eliza (Warrups) Mauwee
Requesting the permission of the General Assembly to sell lands inherited from her father and possessed in right of Eliza so that they can purchase land in Cornwall where they now reside. Sherman Boardman of New Milford was appointed by the General Assembly to act on the behalf of the petitioners for the sale and purchase.

1799 Indian Papers ser.2, v.II:58 Petition of the Natives at Scattecuk
As a result of a "meting of the Natives" the asked that no more reservation lands be sold to settle debts. It was signed by:
Joseph Mauwee
John Peters
Peter Sherman
Daniel Sucknucks
Elihu Mauwee
Isaack Sucknucks
Job Sucknucks
Danielson Mauwee
Abraham Kunkpot
Levi Succonnucks
Peter Mauwee
Jonas Cocshure

1800 Indian Papers ser.2,v.II :64, Order of the General Assembly
The General Assembly responded by appointing a committee that in turn recommend the sale of lands to settle the Schaghticoke's outstanding debts. Lands at the southernmost end of the reservation to be sold.

1801 Indian Papers ser.2,v.II :66, Petition to the General Assembly by Abraham Fuller, overseer of the Schaghticoke

"The number of Indians has been gradually decreasing, and at this time, amounts to no more than thirty five. These are without exception addicted to intoxication & idleness in an extreme degree and are adverse to every kind of labour. They do not in general attempt to cultivate more than about six acres of land in a year, & this they manage in a very negligent manner. From their habits of living they have been for several years past much more afflicted with sickness than formerly, and the expenses of making necessary provision for them, have been consequently encreased. The lands which the Indians do not cultivate, although let out & managed to the best advantage under the circumstances, produce but a partial provision for defraying their expenses: Being in a situation to be let from year to year, under the incumerances of the Indians residing on any part they choose the lands are daily becoming of less value
 the fences are much decayed, and fifteen pounds per year is the most that can be obtained for the use of the lands. From these circumstances a debt of about one hundred + twenty pounds has already accured, and the rent of the lands is in no wise adequate to the payment of the interest on the debt, & furnishing necessities for those Indians who are unable to furnish themselves."

1801 Financial Statement of the Avails of Scatacook Lands
   cash for building six wigwams 19.74

1801 Connecticut Public Records:315 (October)
   This Assembly Do appoint Mr. Abel Beach to be Overseer of the Scaticook tribe of Indians during the pleasure of this Assembly.

1801 Cornwall Land Records v.7 :334
   Conveyance in fee Hezeriah Gold to Sherman Boardman Esq.trustee for Eliza Warrups, Charles Mauwee Oct.3 1801

1801 Schaghticoke Reservation, Abel Beach
   Jonus (Cockshure) (Living with wife (Lydia) at La Grange, Dutchess County New York c.1790)
Overseer provided: leather for mocasins to Jonas

1802 Schaghticoke Reservation, Abel Beach
   Nelda (Hulda Keehore)
   Sarah Phillips

Johanna
Sarah Suckernuck
Jemima Suckernuck
Gideon (Sherman) (*living in Dover New York*)
Sybbell (**death**)
Jonas (Cockshure)
   Overseer provided: shoes, food, and burial necessities (candles, rum, coffin, horse & wagon to transport body). Had to procure a horse to bring Gideon back from Dover NY. Medical expenses.

1803 Schaghticoke Reservation, Abel Beach
Sarah (Phillips?)
Sarah Suckernuck (*from Sherman*) (death)
Old Anna
Nuldy (Hulda Keehore) (*from Armenia New York*) (death)
Kate (Suckernuck?) (**death**)
James (death)
Joe (Mauwee?)
Old Sarah (Mauwee ?)
   Overseer provided: shoe repair, Medical expenses, transportation of ill tribe members from Sherman and Armenia, deed preparation, leather, burial necessities
wrapping cloth, candles, rum and coffin wagon and horse, firewood. Schooling being provided at cost to Indian children.

1803 April, Indian Papers ser.2,v.II:71, Accounts of Overseer of the Scatacook Tribe of Indians
   "Scatacook tribe of Indians to Abel Beach, Overseer To Indians, from Oct 1st 1801 to March 1st 1803 being necessary articles of clothing, Physician bills, expenses in sickness, Overseers time & trouble, Committee expenses +c.

	Dol 140.60
To balance in overseers hands	80.10
	Dol 220.70

1803 May, Indian Papers, ser.2,v.II:72 Petition of Joseph Pratt
   "...That at a session of the Genl Assembly at New Haven on the secnd Thrusday of Oct 1792 he was appointed Overseer to Joseph Mauwe Jemima Suckanux, +David Suckanux, Indians residing in Scatacook, with directions to take care of their Estates—That the said Joseph Mauwee is since dead, leaving Elihu Mauwee his son + heir, And that there is a sum of money now belonging to sd indians—The memorialist would represent that by reason of ill health he is unable any longer to manage + the Estates

of sd Indians + would pray your Honors/ to dismiss him from further serving as overseer to sd Indians…"

Joseph Mauwee was married to Sarah.

These individuals were residing at Derby (Seymour) in 1792 (see Indian Paperas ser. 2,v.II:51). The general Assembly dismissed Pratt and assigned them to Abel Beach.

1804 Schaghticoke Reservation, Abel Beach.

Joanna

Mima

Old Sarah (Mauwee)

Peter Sherman (*living away from Schaghticoke: Dover, New York 1817 rpt.*)

Benj. Chickens (rec.$100 per CT. General Assembly order) [see Indian Papers, ser.2,v.II:75, May 1801]

Eunice

Agnes

Betsey **(death)**

Child (death)

Thom Wallops

Overseer provided: leather for mocasons, shoes, medical expenses, transportation of ill members, non-Indian care of ill members, plowing, fencing & gardening by non-member, burial necessities coffin, wrapping cloth, candles , cutting & drawing wood.

1805 Schaghticoke Reservation, Abel Beachh

Old John

Old John & Joanna

Bill Keehore

Sarah (taking care of John & Joanna)

Gideon Sherman (*from Dover New York*)

Ann's child **(death)**

Vina **(death)**

Mimi's child **(death)**

Overseer provided: cutting & drawing wood, payment for use of burying ground, physical care of members, paid care of ill members by non-members, paid care of ill members by other members, medical care, leather, providing non-member midwife, leather, burial necessities (winding cloths, rum, candles, coffin, transportation). Provisions (meats, cheese, pork, flower, tabacco), cloathing

1806 Schaghticoke Reservation, Abel Beach
Joanna (**death**)
Peter (Mauwee?)
Tom &John
Daniel Suckernuck (received interest on John Hopkins note (lease?)
Betsey
Old John
Eunice
Her mother
James (death)
Peter Mauwee
Benj Chickens

Overseer provided: wood, burial necessities (coffin, candles, rum, cloth, transportation), expenses for use of burial ground, clothing, care of ill member (mother) by a member (daughter/ Eunice), provisions (corn, pork, bread, chickens).

1807 Schaghticoke Reservation, Abel Beach
Peter Mauwee
Benj Chickens
Old Sarah
Jonas (**death**)

Overseer provided: provisions, clothing, tools (Sarah, a hatchett), medical, leather, payment for use of burial ground, wood, plowing of gardens by non-members, schooling expenses.

1808 Schaghticoke Reservation, Abel Beach
Old John & Ann
Jonas (Dutchess County New York) (**death**)
Benj Warrups children
Peter (Mauwee)
Laura
Sarah

Overseer provided: medical assistance, payment for use of burial ground, plowing by non-member, wood, leather for shoes, transportation of ill member.

1809 Schaghticoke Reservation
Ned's children (schooling)
Benj Chickens children (schooling)
Eunice & Sarah
Old Sarah

Laura
Betsey **(death)**
Old John **(death)**
Elihu (injury **(death)**
Abraham Rice's children (schooling)
Peter (Mauwee?)

Overseer provided: Medical assistance, payment for use of burial ground, surveying of reservation south boundary, plowing by non-member, clothing, burial necessities
winding clothes, whiskey, coffin.

1810 Schaghticoke Reservation, Abel Beach
Old Sarah **(death) (Mauwee)**
Abraham Rice's children
Joe (*transport from Jason Wings to resv.*)

Overseer provided: Burial necessities (grave cloths, coffin transportation), medical assistance, transportation of ill member, plowing by non-member, midwife visit.

1811 Schaghticoke Reservation
Abraham Rice
B. Chicken
Eunice & child (son)
Job
Margr (*trans to resv.*)
Jacobs child **(death)**
Dennis (death)
Widow Sarah
Pol (*trans to resv. from Jo Thomas res.*)
Sarah Mauwee **(death)** (*residing at W. Dunkin re*s.)
Mrs Mowrey
Jerry (Mauwee?)(*in Warren*)
Jacob (Mauwee)
Benj Chicken

Overseer provided: shoe mending, medical assistance, payment for use of burial ground, schooling, plowing and railing by non-member, reservation survey, care of ill member by non-member, wood, transportation of ill members, burial necessities (coffins, winding cloths, burial), nails, Bible.

1812 Schaghticoke Reservation, Abel Beach
> B. Chicken
> Joe Bean
> Jerry
> Jacob Mauwee
> Wm Keehore (*res. of Elijah Gaylord*)
> Rachel **(death)**
> Peter Sherman (*from Dover New York*) **(death)**
> Rice
> (winding cloths, brandy, coffin), medical assistance, new log house, boarding, nails, payment for use of burying ground, transportation of member (Peter's body from Dover).

1812 Barzillai Slossom, History of Kent
> "The present number [1812] of Indians is about forty."
> Slossom gave no details concerning the contemporary situation of the Schaghticoke community.

1812 Act of the General Assembly
> Oliver Burnham appointed conservator over Jeremiah Coxil, Rufus Bunker, Peter Mauwee Indians of Cornwall, children of Eliza Warrups alias Mauwee

1812 Cornwall Land Records v.9:469
> Land Conveyance in fee Oliver Burnham et. al. trustee to Theron & Elizabeth Coltin Oct. 3, 1812

1813 Schaghticoke Reservation, Abel Beach
> Abrigail (*to resv. From Elijah Warner res.*)
> Sarah **(death)**
> Keehore (William)
> Jean **(death)**
> Daniel (death)
> Benj Chickens
> Joseph Mauwee **(death)** (*res. In Warren*)
> Mima (*at Gaylordsville*)
> Old Jemima (Suckernucks) **(death)** (*res. off resv.* Wm. Chapman)
> Overseer provided: School (Rice/Chickens children), medical assistance, care of member by non-member, burial necessities (grave clothes, coffin), plowing by non-member, transportation of body (Joseph Mauwee) from Warren/ (Jemima) from Chapman res.), caring for ill member by a member (paid).

1814 Schaghticoke Reservation, Abel Beach
 Joseph Mauwee Children (*from Warren*)
 Dennis
 Martin
 Jacobs family
 Child (Mauwee?)
 Benj Chicken
 Peter Hine (**death**)
 (Joe) Mauwee child
 Abrigail
 Eunice
 Taber Mauwee
 Charlotte
 Jeremiah Tomuck (*in res.Judge Barrows*)
  Overseer provided: transportation of Mauwee children from Warren by member, care of members by non-member, care of member by member, medical assistance, plowing by non-member, transportation of member, Schooling, burial (clothes, coffin).

1814   Order of the General Assembly

Resolved by this Assembly that the overseer of the Scanticook tribe of Indians be and he is hereby appointed Guardian to the orphan Children belonging to sd. tribe of Indians

1815 Schaghticoke Reservation, Abel Beach
 David (**death**)
 Polly Cockshure (**death**)
 Chicken
 Abrigail
 Child (*buried in New Milford*)
 A. Rice
  Overseer provided: schooling (Chickens, Rice), burial necessities (burial clothes, winding clothes, brandy, coffins), provisions (rye for Chickens), medical assistance, plowing, providing wood.

1816 Schaghticoke Reservation
 Jacob Mauwee (received cash)
 Margery (*res. New Milford*)
 Isaac (Rogers) (**death**)

Overseer provided: medical assistance, transportation of off-resv. member (Margery), schooling, burial necessities (clothes, coffin).

1817 Schaghticoke Reservation, Abel Beach
Jerry Tomuck (Jeremiah) (*res. off resv. Ewesworth*)
N. Rice
J. Mauwee (settling accounts,expenses) **(death?)** (Joseph?)
Eunice & J. Tomack
Benj Chickens
Taber (Mauwee)
Elihu (rtn. to resv. 34 miles)
Job's family
Overseer provided: medical assistance, transportation of members, provide shoes, provide school book, provide wood, plowing by non-member, member being paid to care for member, non-member caring for member, schooling.

(No 1818 Schaghticoke Reservation Account, Abel Beach)

1819 Schaghticoke Reservation, Abel Beach
A. Rice
Jere Tomucks family (*in New Milford*)
Eunice & Tomuck
Old Eunice Wallops
Gid Sherman & wife (*from New Milford*)
Rhoda (death)
Eunice
Gid. Child
Overseer provided: wood, schooling, transportation of member back to resv., plowing by non-member, clothing, provisions, burial necessities (grave cloths, coffin), nails.

1820 Schaghticoke Reservation, Abel Beach
Moses Smith of Armenia (for keeping Indians when sick)
A. Rice
Miah child **(death)**
Gid (Gideon Mauwee) (*res. off resv.*)
Job (death)
Joe Penee **(death)** (res. in Newtown)
E. Wallops
Wallops family

Overseer provided: medical assistance, cloth, schooling (Rice), Burial necessities (Clothing, coffin), non-members caring for members, plowing, paying of funeral charges to Newtown.

1821 Schaghticoke reservation, Abel Beach
Eunice Job
Benj Chickens child **(death)**
Eunice's child **(death)**
Gideon Sherman **(death)** (*res. New Milford*)
Laura **(death)**
Peter Hine **(death)**
Benjm Chickens
Miah child
Ned Rice daughter
Paid Dr. Shelton of Stratford
Paid Dr. Chitteden (*Cornwall?*)

Overseer provided: schooling, clothing, burial necessities (burial clothes,coffin), medical assistance, plowing by non-member, Bible, care of ill member by non-member, wood.

1822 Schaghticoke reservation, Abel Beach
Miah's child **(death)**
J. Tomock (*res. Bridgeport*)
Jacob Mauwee
Eunice & Abrigail
Ned's child **(death)** (Ned Rice)
Peter Mauwee **(death)**
Benj Chickens family
Benj Chickens
Eunice & children (*res. George Bull*)
Benj Chickens child **(death)**
  Paid Dr. Chittendens bill (*Cornwall?*)

Overseer provided: schooling, medical assistance, burial necessities (grave clothes, coffin), transportation of member from Bridgeport, provisions, court fees, plowing by non-member.

1822, Cornwall, Town Accounts: Anson Rogers, Collector, To a Town Tax or Rate Bill delivered to him to Collect made on the List of Cornwall for the Year 1822
55 by selectman Order J. Coxil Aug 19 1822 21.69

1823 Schaghticoke reservation, Abel Beach
Ned Rice Children
Child (**death**) (Ned Rice?)
Ned Rice children (2 graves)
Benj Chicken
Eunice
Taber (Mauwee)
John Mauwee
Isaac Rogers
Abraham Peters child (**death**)
Ned Rice
Overseer provided: schooling, burial necessities (Coffin, grave clothes), plowing by non-member, nails, timber, paying member to care for member, calling for ill member by non-member, provisions.

1823 Cornwall: James Wadsworth Collector To Town Tax or Rate Bill delivered to him to Collect taxed on the List of the Town of Cornwall for the Year 1823
#16 By Selectman Order J. Coxil Dec 21st 1823 5.33
#42 By Selectman Order J. Coxil March 17th 1823 6.00

1824 Schaghticoke reservation
Polly (Pan) (*trans. to resv.*), (*from Cornwall?*)
Miah (**death**)
Taber (Mauwee)
Wm Cockshure (res. off resv. Danl Turrell)
Polly Pan
Walters child
Paid Dr. Chittenden (*Cornwall?*)
Overseer provided: transportation to resv. of ill member, burial necessities (colthes, coffin), wood, care of ill member by non-member, medical assistance, provisions, Bible, spelling book.

1825 Schaghticoke reservation, Abel Beach
Old Sue (from Bridgeport) (Tomock?)
Sarah Chickens
Old Squaws
Abrigail
Polly (Pan?)
Abraham (Peters)
Eunice
Lavinia (death)

Nehemiah

Overseer provided: repairs to Indian huts by non-member, cutting & drawing wood, transportation of member from Bridgeport, provisions, member paid to take care of member, schooling, caring of member by non-member, clothing.

1826 Schaghticoke reservation, Abel Beach

Eunice
Old Sue
Walter
Old Abrigail
Doctor Turners *Acct of Cornwall*
Elihu *(Newtown)*
John Suckernuck (*Newtown*)

Overseer provided: cutting & carting wood, paid a member for caring for a member, schooling, medical assistance, plowing.

1827 Schaghticoke reservation, Abel Beach

John (res. *off resv. Mary McDuff*)
Abrigail
Sally Rice (*res. off resv. Marvin Smith*)
Eunice (res. off resv. James Beardsley)
B. Chickens family
A. Chickens child (**death**)
Moses Rice (**death**)
Polly (Pan) (res off resv Curtiss Hallocks) (**death**)
Ned Rrice daughter (**death**)
Ned Rice son & daughter (**death**)
Jerry Tomuck & family (*from Norwalk*)

Overseer provided: non-member taking care of member, transporting member to resv., schooling, provisions, wood, boards, nails, repair of house by non-member, burial necessities.

1828 Schaghticoke reservation, Abel Beach

Chickens
Moses Rice (**death**)
Eunice
Polly
Benj Chickens (**death**)
Ned Rice daughter (**death**)
Ned Rice son (**death**)
Abrigail

Jerry Tomuck & family (*from Norwalk*)
Indian boy (*from Bridgewater*)
Overseer provided: shoe mending, burial necessities (coffin , vinegar, grave clothes), transportation of members to resv., medical assistance, wood, provisions.

1829 Schaghticoke reservation Schaghticoke reservation, Abel Beach
Abigail
Indian children
Eunice
Sarah (Chickens?)
Sarah Chickens
Overseer provided: wood, medicine, schooling, shoe mending, provisions, medical assistance, hut repairs, care of member by non-member.

1830 Schaghticoke reservation, Abel Beach
Taber (Mauwee)
Ned Rice
John Mauwee (*res. off resv. Martin Preston*)
Eunice
Fear
Fear's child (**death**)
Nancy Chickens
Jeremiah Tomuck
Abrigail
Sarah Chickens (*from Pines Plains*)
Overseer provided: medical assistance, schooling (Ned Rice fam.), transportation of ill member to resv., plowing by non-member, burial necessities(cloth, coffin), provisions, wood, hut repairs.

1831 Schaghticoke reservation, Abel Beach
Abraham (Peters) (**death**)
James (*res. in Newtown*)
Wm Cockshure (trans. to resv. Six miles) (**death**)
Sarah Chickens
Tamar
Rice
Overseer provided: burial necessities (clothes, coffin), transportation of member to resv., keeping member by non-member, member paid to care for member, medical assistance, schooling (Rice), cutting & drawing wood for three huts by non-member.

1832 Schaghticoke reservation, Abel Beach
  Abrigail **(death)**
  Rachel (*in Woodbridge*)
  Wm Cocksure (*res. at Wm Turrells, 6 miles from resv.*)
  Child (death)
  *Doctor Hollisters bill for doctoring Cornwall Indi*ans
  Taber (Mauwee)
  Overseer provided: burial necessities (clothes, coffin), transportation
of members back to resv., cutting & sledding wood by non-member,
medical assistance, medical payments for Indians in Cornwall.

1833 Schaghticoke reservation, Abel Beach
  J Mauwe
  Julia Rice **(death)**
  Overseer provided: Schooling, medical assistance, provide timber,
plowing by non-member, burial necessities (coffin).

1834 Schaghticoke reservation, Abel Beach
  John Suckernucks (*to Onieda New York*)
  Fear (death)
  Taber Mauwee (*res. in Litchfield, rtn. to resv.*) **(death)**
  Overseer provided: medical assistance, burial necessities (digging
grave, shroud, burial clothes,), plowing by non-member, transportation of
member to resv, (Taber from Litchfield).

1835 Schaghticoke reservation, Abel Beach
  Tamer (*res. Spencer Hitchcock, in Warren*) **(death)**
  Martha Mauwee (*res. Russell Mallory in Northville*)
  Patty Mauwee (*res. Noah Bartram*)
  Lavinia
  Albert
  Angeline **(death** *at New Milford*)
  Eunice (mentioned in 1836 as res. on resv. this year)
  Overseer provided: Schooling, cutting & drawing wood, non-
memmber caring for member, transportation of members, burial necessities
(shroud, coffin), paying funeral/medical expenses to Sharon, paying
member to care for member, medical assistance, paid funeral/medical
expenses to New Milford.

1835 September, Cornwall, Petition of James Wadsworth of Cornwall to the Litchfield County Court.

"Whereas Oliver Burnham Esqr. Of Cornwall in Litchfield County was by this Assembly in May 1812, authorized and empowered to sell certain lands belonging to Jerimiah Coxil, Rufus Bunker, and Peter Mauwee, Indians, children heirs of late Eliza Warrups Chickens, alias Mauwee then late of said Cornwall deceased, that said lands have been sold by the said Oliver Burnham & that part of the avails thereof belonging to the said Jeremiah Coxil now remain in the hands of said Burnham, which ought to be kept and expended for the said Coxils, maintence. Therefore Resolved by this Assembly that James Wadsworth Esqr. of Cornwall be & is hereby appointed an agent to receive all money and other estate if any now in the hands of said Burnham or others and belonging to said Coxil and expend the same for his support under the direction of Litchfield Court..."

In September of 1835 Burnham transferred to Wadsworth the sum of two hundred and sixty-nine dollars and thirty-six cents belonging to Coxil. The County Court directed Wadsworth that he could only use money derived from the interest acquired on this money not to exceed thirty dollars a year and that he was to submit a report of all expenses in 1836.

1836 Schaghticoke reservation, Abel Beach
John Mauwee (*res. Gilbert Smith of Warren*) (rtn. to resv.)
O. Chickens (**death**)
Henry Rice (**death**)
    Overseer provided: cutting & drawing wood, payment to non-member for caring for member (Gilbert Smith),transportation of member to reservation, provisions, plowing by non-member, schooling, paid member to care for member, burial necessities (coffin), construct two dwelling houses on resv.

1837 Schaghticoke reservation, Abel Beach
Pd Dr. Huxley's bill to James Wadsworth (Cornwall)
Adonijah Cogswell (**death**) (j. Bartram digging grave (*Cornwall?*)
Wido Cogshall
Jim
Tomuck (**death**)
Nancy Chickens (**death**) (*off reservation*)
H. Rice (**death**)
Patty Mauwee (*res Elijah Gaylord*)
Child (**death**)

Overseer provided: Burial necessities (digging grave,coffin), provide wood, clothing, medical assistance, pd for medical assistance to Cornwall, non member paid for caring for member, paid funeral charges (N. Chickens).

1838 Schaghticoke reservation, Abel Beach
Old Eunice
Charles Mauwee (**death** *in Sharon*)
Overseer provided: wood, medical assistance, plowing by non-member, paid funeral expenses to Sharon.

1839 Schaghticoke reservation
Old Eunice
David
Albert
Overseer provided: non-member paid to care for member, plowing by non-member, drawing fence rails by non-member, provisions, paid member to care for member.

1840 Schaghticoke reservation, Abel Beach
Alma child (death)
Old Eunice
Overseer provided: paid medical expenses to Cannan, burial necessities (shroud,coffin), drawing rails, making fence, plowing, provisions, schooling.

1840 Cornwall Land Records v.14:370
Land Conveyance in fee Daniel Bunker to Daniel Tomlinson Jan. 31, 1840, v.14:274
Land Conveyance in fee Samuel Stirling to Rufus Bunker Oct. 23 1840, v.14:275
Land Conveyance in fee Rufus Bunker to Daniel Bunker Oct. 23, 1840

1841 Schaghticoke reservation, Abel Beach
J. Mauwee (John?) (res. Blackman) (*rtn to resv.*)
Elihu Mauwee (sick / lame, brought back to resv. *from Wethersfield*)
Patty Mauwee (*in Northville*)
Overseer provided: medical assistance, schooling, plowing, drawing rails, paid non-member to care for member, transportation of member back to resv., non-member paid to care for member, build house on resv. by non member (Root).

1842 Schaghticoke reservation, Abel Beach
Roxa (**death** *in Cornwall*)
Jacob Mauwee
Old Eunice
Abraham Lee
Abrigail
Joseph Mauwee
Elihu
Doctr Scovills Acct against Cogshall (*Cornwall*)
Overseer provided: paid funeral expenses to Cornwall, provisions, clothing, wood, shoes and boots, paid Joseph Mauwee to cut wood.

1842 Cornwall Town Records, Deaths, Births, Marriages, v.3:64
Eli Bunker of Cornwall married Fannie Mae Walker of Glastonbury Feb. 9 1842

1843 Schaghticoke reservation, Abel Beach
Julia Kilson
Jacob Mauwee
Child (**death**)
Eunice
James Wadsworth for support of Cornwall Indians
Overseer provided: cloth, sowing (Jacob Mauwee), shoes, leather, clothing, burial necessities (shroud, coffin), payment to Cornwall, medical assistance, plowing, shingles and nails,.

1843 Cornwall, Town Accounts
Paid Order #44 to J. Coxil dated Nov 20th 43 2.21

1844 Schaghticoke reservation, Abel Beach
Old Eunice
Alexander (**death**)
Abraham Lee
Alma
Patty
Rachel
Jacob Mauwee
Truman Mauwee (Bradley)
John Mauwee
A.V. Kilson
Joseph Mauwee

Overseer provided: Medical assistance, plowing (Jacob Mauwee), burial necessities (digging grave), shoes (4 pr.), provisions (corn, flour), pd. hand sled (by Jacob Mauwee), pd. cutting wood (Jacob Mauwee), pd. butchering cow (Jacob Mauwee), clothes, pd.hoeing corn (Jacob Mauwee), (Truman Bradly (cited as Mauwee) began work in July, pd. plowing corn (Abijah), pd. shoe repairs (Truman Bradley), pd. John Mauwee work haying, pd. A.V. Kilson for butchering,

1844 Connecticut Court Records, Litchfield County Judicial District
Arrin Cogshall note $1000 Indian paid to Jan 1st 1845

1845 Schaghticoke reservation, Abel Beach
Vina
Joseph Mauwee
A.v. Kilson
Truman Indian (Bradley)
Joseph Mauwee
Julia Kilson
Overseer provided: pd. Jacob Mauwee, A.V. Kilson, John Mauwee butchering, provisions, pd. Truman Bradley work (23 days), pd. Joseph Mauwee work (hoeing corn), pd. A.V. Kilson work, pd. Julia Kilson work (18 weeks).

1846 Schaghticoke reservation, Abel Beach
Eunice
A.V. Kelson
Truman Bradley
Elihu Mauwee
John Mauwee
Overseer provided: provisions, wood for Eunice, thrashing wheat (pd. A.V. Kilson), wood for Eunice (pd. Truman Bradley), plowing for Eunice & Rachel by non-member, repair roof /fix house Butchering Heifer (pd. Truman Bradley), shoe thread, Rye, cutting wood (pd. Truman Bradley), clothes, planting corn (pd. John Mauwee, Elihu Mauwee, Truman Bradley), plowing corn (pd. Truman Bradley, Elihu Mauwee), hoeing corn (pd. A.V. Kelson, Elihu Mauwee), thrashing buckwheat, husking corn, butchering Heifer, hogs (pd. A.V. Kilson, Truman Bradley), thrashing oats (pd. Truman Bradley), cutting wood (pd. Truman Bradley), raking wheat and mowing (pd. Truman Bradley, haying (pd. Elihu Mauwee)

1847 Schaghticoke reservation, Abel Beach

Rachel (Mauwee)
Eunice
Child (**death**)
Parmelia (Mauwee)
Sophronia
Jacob Mauwee
Truman Bradley
Elihu Mauwee
A.V. Kelson
John Mauwee

Overseer provided: medical assistance, tools, cutting & drawing wood, burial necessities, plowing, construction of dwelling house, produce, leather goods, drawing wood on sled (pd. Truman Bradley), cutting wood (pd. Truman Bradley), hoeing corn (pd. Truman Bradley), haying (pd. Truman Bradley, A.V. Kilson), thrashing buckwheat (pd. Alexander V. Kilson), picking corn (pd. A.V. Kilson, John Mauwee), A.V. Kilson for keeping 2 hogs 2 months, butchering cow/hogs (pd. Truman Bradley), cutting & pitching wood for old Eunice (pd. Truman Bradley, A.V. Kilson).

1848 Schaghticoke reservation, Abel Beach

Cogshall (*of Cornwall*) (to pay rail expenses) (also delivered goods from overseer to Cornwall)
Old Eunice
Truman & Joe (*to New Haven)*
Parmelia
Patty Mauwee (*living in New Milford*)
Jacob Mauwee (living in Milford, rtn to resv.) (**death**)
Truman Bradley
A.V. Kilson
J. Cogswall – *Cornwall* (**death**)
Eunice (**death**-*Milford*)
Patty Mauwee (*New Milford)*

Overseer provided: medical assistance, clothing , boots, bulk fabric, cutting & carting wood, transportation (to New Haven, to Cornwall by members), schooling, plowing, care of member by non-member, transportation of member to resv., drawing wood (pd. Joe), plowing & sowing oats (pd. A.V. Kilson), planting potatoes (pd. Truman Bradley), plowing with oxen (pd. Truman Bradley), seeding (pd. A.V. Kilson), plowing with oxen (pd. Truman Bradley), plow corn with horse (Truman Bradley, A.V. Kilson), brush removal (pd. Truman Bradley), plow amoung

corn & buckwheat (pd. Joe), 4 days work (pd. Truman Bradley), haying
(pd. A.V. Kilson), mowing & carting meadow grass (pd. Truman Bradley
& Joe), harvesting hay and oats (pd. Truman Bradley), raking buckwheat
(pd. Truman Bradley), thrashing buckwheat (pd. Truman Bradley), husking
corn (pd. Truman Bradley), butchering heifer (pd. Truman Bradley).

1849 Schaghticoke reservation, Abel Beach
   Elihu
   Laura
   Julia (Bradley)
   Old Eunice
   Truman Bradley
   Overseer provided: wood, cloth, leather, transportation of injured
member back to resv., non-members paid to care for members, schooling,
plowing, medical assistance, Cutting wood (pd. Truman Bradley), plowing
& drawing rails (pd. Truman Bradley, pasturing cow (pd. Truman
Bradley), plowing, brush removal, ground buckwheat (pd. Truman
Bradley), Horse and wagon 13 miles to Sharon (Truman Bradley).

1849 Cornwall Town Records, Deaths ,Births, Marriages v.3:106-107
   Benjamin Bunker, laborer, died July 19,1849,ae 40

1849 Cornwall Town Records, Deaths, Births, Marriages v.3:83
   Emily Coggswell of Cornwall married A.L. Rogers of New Milford
Nov.29 1849 North Congregational Church

1850 (Smallpox) Schaghticoke reservation, Abel Beach
   Rachel (*trans .to resv.*)
   Eliza
   Truman Bradley
   Value A. Kilson
   Alexander V. Kilson
   John Mauwee
   Caroline
   Abram
   Elihu
   Harvey
   Joab
   Overseer provided: medical assistance (smallpox), schooling,
provisions, keeping and fetching Rachel by non-member, drawing wood
(pd. Truman Bradley), plowing (pd. Truman Bradley), sowing oats (pd.
Truman Bradley), grinding rye (pd. Truman Bradley), sowing rye (pd.

Truman Bradley), pasturing cow 22 weeks (pd. Alexander Kilson), draw two loads of cornstalk from Truman corn lot (pd. Alexander V. Kilson), butcher Heifer/hogs (pd. Truman Bradley), threshing wheat (pd. A.V. Kilson, Truman Bradley). mowing (pd. John Mauwee), hoeing (pd. John Mauwee), haying (pd. A.V. Kilson), grass mowing (pd. Truman Bradley).

1851 Order of the Superior Court Litchfield County to Edward Smith MD of Cornwall

You are hereby notified that the undersigned will meet you on the 22nd day of February 1851 at the dwelling house of Abel Beach of Kent in said County for the purpose of examining your account against the said Beach as Conservator of the Scatacook tribe of Indians for medical services rendered the family of Jeremiah Coggswell deceased represented as belonging to said Tribe...

1851 Schaghticoke reservation, Abel Beach

Eliza
A.V. Kilson
Truman Bradley
Payment to Cornwall Selectmen
Joe & Parelia
Old Eunice
Joe Kilson
John Mauwee
Parmelia
Old John
Value (Kilson)

Edward Smith M.D. mtg. Abel Beach for services in Cornwall to Jeremiah Cogswell **(deceased)** and family.

Mary Jane Kilson
Mary Beach
Nancy
Laura
Laura's child **(death)**

Overseer provided: medical assistance, schooling, furniture, burial necessities (shroud & coffin), sawing, shingles & nails, lime, oak board, shingling & repairing house, provisions, calico, boots, payment to miller, plowing hoe, drawing fence, construction of dwelling, butcher/ dress heifer/hogs (pd. A.V. Kilson), thrashing rye (pd. A.V. Kilson, Truman Bradley), drawing wood (pd. Truman Bradley), gathering hay (pd. A.V. Kilson, Truman Bradley, Joseph Kilson), work at stone wall (pd. Truman Bradley), work at stone (pd. A.V. Kilson), drawing stalks (pd. Truman

Bradley), laying stone wall (pd. A.V. Kilson), draw stone and logs to saw mill (pd. A.V. Kilson), cutting apple trees (pd. A.V. Kilson, Mary Jane Kilson began work.

1852 Schaghticoke reservation, Abel Beach
Truman Bradley
A.V. Kilson
Joseph Kilson
Abrigail
Eunice
Ned

Overseer provided: cutting trees (pd. Truman Bradley), thrashing oats (pd. Truman Bradley), butcher hogs (pd. A.V. Kilson), digging & drawing stone (pd. Truman Bradley), sowing plaster (pd. A.V. Kilson), plowing (pd.Truman Bradley), planting corn (pd. Truman Bradley), plow & harrow (pd. A.V. Kilson), haying (pd. A.V. Kilson, Truman Bradley), thrashing buckwheat (pd. Truman Bradley), drawing corn stalks (pd. Joe and Truman Bradley), butcher hogs (pd. Truman Bradley).

1852 Cornwall Land Records v.18:10

Conveyance in fee James Wadsworth to Nathan Coggswell April 15, 1852

1853 Schaghticoke reservation, Abel Beach
Truman Bradley
Joseph Kelson
A.V. Kilson
Truman's wife
Abram
Elihu's wife
Elihu
Eunice
Caroline
Parmelia

By interest paid on note of Swift's of Cornwall

Overseer provided: shoes, clothing, nails, shingles for John's house, cloth provisions, help butcher beef (pd. Truman Bradley), pd. Joseph Kilson balance for one year's work, trimming trees (pd. Truman Bradly), hoeing corn (pd. Joseph Kilson), cradling wheat (pd. Joseph Kilson), cradling and securing grain (pd. Joseph Kilson), haying (pd. Joseph Kilson), picking corn (pd. Joseph Kilson).

1853 Cornwall Land Records v.19:194
Conveyance in fee Nathan Coggswell from Isaac Wetherly Dec.1, 1853

1854 Schaghticoke reservation, Abel Beach
Joseph Kilson
Truman Bradley
A.V. Kilson
Overseer provided: paid fine & cost on the Newtown case, provisions, help butcher hogs (pd. A.V. Kilson), keeping cow six months (pd. Joseph Kilson), help butcher hogs (pd. Truman Bradley, A.V. Kilson), plowing garden (pd. A.V. Kilson), cutting corn (pd. Truman Bradley), butchering heifer (pd. A.V. Kilson), work on school house (pd. A.V. Kelson)

A Chronological Listing of Schaghticoke Related Store and Overseer Accounts, 1823-1854

1823-1824 Skiff & Goodsell Account Book

August-October 1823 **Benjamin Chickens**
Lamb, Rye, Molasses
January-July 1824 Benjamin Chickens
B-Salts, Braids, Butter, goods, watch

July 1824 **Nancy Chickens**
Duck feathers

1830-1840 Daniel Morehouse Account Book

May-June 1838 **Jacob Mauwee**.
By day laboring "on the bush" $7.34

July 1838 **Jacob Mauwee**
By day laboring "on the bush"

November 1838 **Jacob Mauwee**
Purchase 18 hundred and eighty feet of shingles

1842-1852 Account Book of Abel Beach Overseer.

1842

Jacob Mauwee: Cr, 1 pig for old **Eunice**: 5 lb pig cash 4 qt salt, 4 ¼ lb flour, help butcher 1 heifer **Jacob Mauwee**: 1.50, 4 cords chestnut wood, 1 hat, Taping **Abigal** shoes & **Joe** boots, **Joseph Mawwee**: pd 1 day cutting wood 1 peck corn 1 qt vinegar, ½ bushel corn2 lb pork.

1843

Julia Kilson: goods bought from Goodsell per bill, **Julia Kilson**: 1 cotton spool thread& piece, cotton cloth, 8 yds calico. **Jacob Mauwee**: cr 1 ¾ days sowing pasture 1.17. Jacob Mauwee: 2 bushel [?]. **Julia Kilson**: pr shoes. **Julia Kilson**: leather, for calico dress, apron, to four dollars, to two dollars, to cash .12 ½ , leather for 2 pr shoes, to two dollars, by 39 weeks work 39.00, to cash 8 ½ dollars. Abraham Lee by making shoes for **old Eunice, Alma, Patty' Rachel**. Taping pair shoes **old Eunice**, 1 bushel corn, 2 trees in squaw lot

1844

    Jacob Mauwee: by help butchering heifer .37 ½, 44 lbs beef, by making hand sled .75, 11 ½ lbs flour, cutting wood 4 days 2.00, by cutting wood at door 4 days 2.00, sowing pasture 1 day .50, plowing 2/3 day 1.00, peck corn for seed, powing .75, eight bushels potatoes, hoeing corn 3 days 1.50, hoeing corn 4 days 2.00, 7 yds shirting, cotton spool thread. **Truman Mauwee[Bradley]**: began work July 8, five dollars, leather for caps, leather for 2 pr shoes taps. **Jacob Mauwee**: plowing corn ½ day 1.00, 6 lb pork, **John Mauwee**: 4 ½ lb pork. **Truman Mauwee [Bradley]**: to 2.00, **John Mauwee**: two days work at hay 1.50, peck meal. **Truman Mauwee**: money had of Joe 2.00, .50 for bolt. **John Mauwee**: 1 ½ days work 1.12 ½, tobacco. **Truman Mauwee**: to cash 1.25. **John Mauwee**: 5 days work haying 3.75. **Truman Mauwee**: by 1 month 3 ¾ days 18.31, to cash 3.88. **A V Kilson**: by picking corn 2 ½ days 1.25, 8 lb pork, 8 lb flour, , help butchering heifer .25, cutting wood 1 day .50.

1845

    A V Kilson: by butchering hogs .50, 7 ½ lb flour, to 1.oo, to 3 dollars. **Joseph Mauwee**: by work 3 days1.50, peck corn, vinegar, 16 lb salt beef, ½ lb tea, 2 ½ lbs beef, work three days 1.50,peck corn, vinegar, 16 lb salt beef, ½ lb tea, 2 lb beef. **A V Kilson**: 4 bushels potatoes. **Joseph Mauwee**: hoeing corn three days 1.50, 1 peck meal, 4 lb flour, potatoes. **Truman Bradley**: cash 5 dollars. **A V Kilson**: cash 15 dollars, to 5 dollars. **Truman Bradley:** by work 23 days @ 16.00 per month, to 7 dollars. 9 lbs salt pork, 7 lbs pork. **A V Kilson**: to 15 dollars. **Truman Bradley**: 7 lb pork, meal. **Julia Kilson**: by 18 weeks work @ 6 78.00, silk dress. **A V Kilson**: to 5 dollars. **Truman Bradley**: 14 ½ lbs pork. **A V Kilson:** to cash paid J R Fuller for chairs. Julia Kilson: 7 lb pork, to 6 dollars and 60 cents. **A V Kilson**: to 10 dollars, 7 ½ lbs flour, 1 ¼ lb butter, cash .50, beef, 5 dollars **Joseph Mauwee**: 1 salt shad. **A V Kilson**: 3 lb pork, 6 ½ lb beef, five dollars, 2 balls shoe thread, 1 pig, 1 ½ bush rye, 7 lb salt beef, by butcher hogs.50, 1 hogs head, 20 lbs pork and beef, by thrashing rye 2 days in dec1.00,1/2 day cutting wood for Eunice.25. **Truman Bradley**: butchering heifer .37 ½ . **A V Kilson** butchering heifer .37 ½, 103 lb beef one quarter. **Truman Bradley**: by cutting wood for Eunice, 8 lb pork. **A V Kilson**: 1 bush rye, by cutting wood 1 day .50, 2 bush rye, 7 lb pork. **Truman Bradley**: 8 lbs pork, cutting wood 2 days 1.00, peck potatoes, cash 2.00, 8 ½ lbs pork, **A V Kilson**: 1 bush potatoes. **Truman Bradley**: 1 knife boughtat Goodsells .37, 30 yds cotton shirting, four dollars, 1 pr taps. **A V Kilson**: 6 qts corn, 5 bush potatoes, 2 bush potatoes, 2 half days sowing pasture .75, sowing pasture. **John Mauwee**:1 ½ days .75. **Elihu Mauwee**: sowing pasture 1 ½ days .75, 6 ½ lb flour, ½ bush potatoes, 5 ¾ lbs pork, cash .25. **John Mauwee**: by planting corn 1 day .50,. Elihu Mauwee: by planting corn 1 day cr. **Truman Bradley**: 2 dollars. **John Mauwee** 2 bush potatoes, plowing 1 day 1.00. **Truman Bradley**: 2 bush potatoes, pr flat irons, cash 3.00, cash .50, 1 salt shad, cash 10.00, 6 ½ lb pork, 11 lb flour, pair & irons, 1 ½ lb cheese. **A V Kilson**: 4 ¾ lb pork. **Elihu Mauwee**: 9 lbs flour. **A V Kilson**: to 3.00. **Truman Bradley**:to 2.00. **Elihu Mauwee**: 1 qt molasses, 12 butter, 6 ½ flour, 2 lb pork, 1 ½ days hoeing corn .75. **A V Kilson**: hoeing 2 days 1.50. **Elihu Mauwee**: 2 lb pork 1 gal soap, 4 lb pork, 32 flour. **A V Kilson**: 5 lbs pork, 1 lb tobacco. **Truman Bradley**: 1 small tub, cash .50, carding 5 lb wool .50. **A V Kilson**: 1 day work at hay 1.00, 3 days work at grain 3.75. **Truman Bradley**: 1 pig, to cash .50, Elihu Mauwee: 1 lb tobacco, 1 knife, .25 cash.

A V Kilson: 1 pr taps, 2 qts vinegar, 1 day work at wheat 1.25, 2 ½ day at hay2.50. **Elihu Mauwee**: 8 lb flour, 3 ¾ pork, 2 qts vinegar, 1 day wheat and mowing cr, 2 days at hay Leonard lot. **Truman Bradley**: 1 pr taps, tacks,3/4 pork, 2 lb veal. **A V Kilson**: piece lamb, 2 lb veal, 4 lb wheat flour. **Elihu Mauwee**: 1 day work at hay cr, A V Kilson: work at hay 2 ¼ days. **Elihu Mauwee**: 3 yds shirting, 4 yds shirting. **A V Kilson**: 1 barrel flour, 4 ¾ lb veal. **Elihu Mauwee**: 2 ¼ lbs pork, 2 qts salt. **Truman Bradley**: to order on Goodsell 2.00. **A V Kilson**: 2 days work at hay2.00. **Elihu Mauwee** 3 ½ days work at hay 2.62, to cash .50. **A V Kilson**: 7 lb 6 oz pork. **Truman Bradley**: to 1.oo. **A V Kilson**: by work 5 days at hay5.00, to cash 3.00. **Elihu Mauwee**: 1 pr boots, 3 days work at hay cr, by 3 days work at hay cr. **Truman Bradley**: to 6.00. **Elihu Mauwee**: 4 lbs pork, 8 lb flour, peck salt, 2 qts vinegar, 7 lbs flour, 3 lbs pork. **A V Kilson**: draw wood 2 days to coal pit1.00, keeping hay 2 months .50. **Elihu Mauwee**: 11 lbs flour, 3 lb pork, 1 gal soap, 2 lb pork. **Truman Bradley**: 2 bush rye, codfish, 1 iron bound keg, piece of beef. **A V Kilson**: thrashing buckwheat ½ day: .25. **Truman Bradley**: 1 bed rope, 1 ½ butter,6 ¼ pork, 9 lbs flour,boots, leather, old feather bed,to cash .50, keg of new cider .30, peck white beans, pieceof beef, 2 bush corn, 1 barrel, load pumpkins 1.00.

A V Kilson: 2 ½ days husking corn1.25,. **Truman Bradley**: to cash .50, two pcs fulled cloth for vest, 6 lb beef, , vest trimming, 1 bush corn, 2 oak boards, trade at Goodsells .50, to cash .25, **by basket.50**, 3 days work 1.50, 1 day thrashing oats .50, to 1.00 cash. **A V Kilson**: help butcher heifer .37 ½, 11 lbs beef, 7 lb ham, help butcher heifer .37 ½, I bush rye. **Truman Bradley**: help butcher heifer .37 ½, 1 bush rye, by butchering hogs .75. **Truman Bradley**: by butchering hogs .75, ½ bush corn, cash .50, taps, by cutting wood 1 day .50, to cash .25, draw load wood .50. **Elihu Mauwee**: 5 ½ lbs pork, peck meal, pork, meal.
1847

Truman Bradley: 2 bush rye, thrashing 35 bush oats 1.05, thrashing 36 ½ bush rye 2.19, 1 peck corn , cash .50, 11 ½ lbs salt beef, 7 yds cotton, 4 ½ lbs codfish, draw wood ½ day .34, thrashing 47 bush oats 1.41. **A V Kilson:** 2 bush rye,. **Truman Bradley:** butchering four hogs 1.00, to cash .50, cash .25, 1 bush corn, thrashing 5 bush rye .30, thrashing 42 bush oats 1.26, thrashing 52 bush rye3.12, 2 bush rye,cash 2.00, corn, cash .62. **Truman Bradley:** pr taps, pair insoles, cutting wood 1 day cr. **Jacob Mauwee: over paid on a basket .12 ½. Truman Bradley:** 1 day cutting wood cr. **Elihu Mauwee: by basket** .25, 4 lbs pork, peck meal. **Truman Bradley:** cash 2.00, bush corn, 1 bush corn, 7 lb 10 oz leather. **A V Kilson:** 2 bush rye. **Truman Bradley:** 2 bush rye, 1/2 day cutting wood .25, draw wood .75, 8 ¼ lb chop, ½ bush potatoes, 1 ½ bush potatoes, 2 bush rye, 1 peck corn, 1 day work .50, ½ daypicking up stone .25, cash .25, 8 lb grease, ½ barrel keg, 1 shad, 5 ½ lb pork, 2 shad, 3 ¼ lb butter, 1 day plowing .50, 13 ½ lbs pork, 1 hoe, 10 bush potatoes, 2 bush rye, 4 ¼ butter, 11 lb chop, 6 ½ veal, plow corn .50, 2 bush rye, molasses, tea. A V Kilson: 6 ½ lb veal. **Truman Bradley:** 4 lb veal, cash 2.00, 2 days hoeing corn 1.50, 2 days work at hay2.00, 1 day at hay 1.00, to cash .25, cash .50, to cash .25, peck potatoes, 9 ¾ lb pork, 2 bush rye, cash 1.00, 1 ½ work w oats/hay 1.50, work athay 1 ½ days 1.50, cash 2.oo, 2 hogs chop. **A V Kilson:** by work ay hay 4 days 4.00. **Truman Bradley:** 2 days work at hay 2.00, 7 lbs pork, 3 lb butter, 12 lbs pork, fresh beef, , 2 bush rye, 1 dollar, 1 lb butter, 7 lbs codfish, 10 ½ pork, to 2.00. **A V Kilson:** thrashing buckwheat ½ day cr. **Truman Bradley:** 8 ¾ pork, 3 bush rye. **A V Kilson:** to 7 ½ bush apples. **Truman Bradley:** 1 gal molasses, 1 load pumpkin 1.00, bushel oats,8 lbs salt pork. By 1 day picking corn cr. **John Mauwee:** by picking corn 3 days 1.50, to cash .25, 5 ½ lb pork, loading manure 2 days1.00, 7 yds shirting, spool thread. A V Kilson: 2 bush corn, 1 bush sheld?, peck meal, 4 lb pork, 2 bush potatoes. **Truman Bradley:** 2 bush rye, butchering cow 37 ½. **A V Kilson** butchering cow .37 ½. **Truman Bradley,** by butchering hogs .50. **A V Kilson:** by butchering hogs paid in corn. **Truman Bradley:** cutting and pitching wood for **old Eunice** .75.

1848

A V Kilson: 1 bush corn, 2 bush rye, cutting wood 4 days 1.87 1/2. **Truman Bradley:**1 bush corn, pr taps. **A V Kilson:** getting wood 3 days 1.50, sowing clover ½ day .30, 1 bush corn, 1pr shoes small, 1 day work at stone cr, ½ day plowing/sowing oats cr, 2 prs taps for wife, 1 bush corn, 1 pr boots, 1 day work, 2 bush rye. **Truman Bradley:** ½ work planting potatoes cr. **A V Kilson:** 2 days work 1.00, plw ½ day .25, 4 lb wool, 10 ½ lbs pork, 2 bush rye. **Truman Bradley:** plow 1 day .50. **A V Kilson:** 2 bush rye, to cash 2.00, 10 lb pork. **Truman Bradley:** ½ day plow corn .50,

2 ½ bush buckwheat. **A V Kilson:** 2 bush rye, 2 bush corn, small wood churn, 8 ¾ pork. **Truman Bradley:** to rub stone, ½ bush potatoes, to 4 dollars, 1 ½ bush rye, 2 bush corn, by work at hay 5 ½ days 5.50, 4 days at work hay 4.00. **A V Kilson:** 2 ½ days at work hay 2.50, 9 ½ lbs pork,1 pr taps. **Truman Bradley:** 4 lb butter. **A V Kilson:** 2 days at work hay 2.00. **Truman Bradley:**4 ½ days work hay 4.50. **A V Kilson:** mowing and carting of meadow grass 7.50. **Truman Bradley:** three days at work hay 3.00, pr taps, 23 lbs pork. **A V Kilson:** 10 ½ lbs pork. **Truman Bradley:** by raking buckwheat 1/3 day .21, husking corn 2 days 1.25, husking corn 2 days 1.25, 1 pr taps, butchering hefer cr, 4 qts salt, 2 bush corn. **A V Kilson:** 8 lbs pork, peck meal. **Truman Bradley:** 2 bush rye, ½ bush corn, 1 day thrashing buckwheat cr, 5 lb pork, 5 lb veal. **A V Kilson:** 8 ½ lbs pork, to 1.00 to 1.00, 9 lb pork, 4 qts salt, 36 lb beef, 2 bush rye.

1849

Truman Bradley: by 1.oo, 1 gal vinegar, 4 bush rye, 1 heifer calf, 2 bush corn, by cutting wood 2 days 2.50, cutting wood 1 day 2.50, 4 bush rye, 1 pig, 2 milk pans, 6 ½ lbs potash, 300 lbs hay, plw and draw rails ½ day 1.00.

Value Kilson: cutting wood 3 days cr. **Truman Bradley:** 3 yds cloth, 1 piece sole leather, to .50, 2 bush rye, 5 ¼ lbs veal, to cash 5.00, pasture for cow 2 weeks.50, plow and bush buckwheat ground 2 ½ days 1.25, 2 bush rye, 18 lbs pork, 2 loads hay, tea, 2 bush rye, peck meal, 11 ½ lbs pork, 12 lb flour, 2 bush rye, pasturing cow 2 weeks .75, 122 lbs beef, 10 lbs tallow, peck salt.

1850

Truman Bradley: 19 lbs beef, butcher hogs ½ day .50, 1 bush salt, 2 50 hay, draw wood 1 day/pair of oxen, by work 1 day cr, to 3.oo, plowing 2 days 1.25, 1 day work sowingoats.62, plow 1 day .75, 12 lbs soap grease, to 2.00, 1 shad, I peck clams, 2 bush potatoes, 1 hoe, to 5.00, 50 lbs wheat flour, 2 pigs, pr taps, to cash 3.00, mowing of meadow grass, 3 bush rye, draw logs to mill 1.50, 10 lb nails, ½ bush buckwheat, 9 ½ pork, 40 ft oak boards, pasturing cow for season 5.00, help butcher heifer .37 ½, help butcher hogs cr, thrashing wheat 5 ½ days. **Value Kilson:** draw wood to mill 1.25, 3 bush corn, 2 bush rye, 5 bush potatoes, 1 bush corn, 2 bush corn, 6 day work at hay cr, fresh beef, 12 days work at hay 12.50, pasturing cow 22 weeks 5.00, 2 bush rye, threshing wheat 5 ½ days 2.75, threshing wheat 5 ½ days cr, 1 qt oil, 2 bush rye.

John Mauwee: to tobacco, cash .50, hoeing corn 1 day 1.00, hoeing corn 1 day cr, to cash .25, by 1 ½ days work at hay1.50

1851

Truman Bradley: thrashing rye 1 day cr, cutting wood at door 4 days cr, cutting wood at door 1 day cr, draw wood 1 day .50, 2 bush corn, 2 bush buckwheat, garden seeds, 8 lbs soap grease, 9 yds calico, pr boots, 1 peck clams, 1 barrel flour, 1 bushel corn, plow 2 half days 1.00, to 10.00, 4 qts salt, by three months work 45.00, 1 ½ days work at stone wall 1.00,1 ½ days work at stone in meadow 1.50, 4 lb old cheese, 1 bush corn,6 lb pig pork.

Value Kilson: , help butcher red heifer .37, help dress 4 hogs cr, thrashing rye 1 day cr, thrashing rye 1 day cr, 3 days cutting wood at door 2.00, 9 ¾ lb pork, 11 ½ lb pork, peck potatoes, by work at hay 13 ½ days cr, 2 ½ days work at oats cr, beef, potatoes, 6 ½ lbs pork, 5 ¾ lb pork,2 bush rye, by work at stone cr, layig stone wall 1 day 1.00, 3 ½ lb pork, cutting apple trees 1 day, bushel corn, 6 lb pork, 2 bush rye, 29 ¼ beef.

Mary Jane Kilson: began work Monday 13th November at 75 cents per week, by work 46 weeks 34.50, Muslin, ribbon, 9 yds lindsy, work on dress and thread, cash paid for stocking yarn, 1 yd calico.

1852

Truman Bradley: cutting apple trees 1 day 1.00, 2 days thrashing oats 1.00,help butcher 4 hogs .50, 4 ¾ lb salt beef, 2 bush corn, by 1.oo paid Bradley, 2 ¾ lb pork, by 1 day digging and drawing stone .62 ½,1 peck seed corn, 2 bush potatoes, 6 ½ lb pork, 1 day planting corn 1.00, plow point, 2 bush rye, 4 ½ lb pork, 1 bushel buckwheat for seed, plow 2 days 1.50, 3 days getting hay 3.75, 1 day do-sick halfprice .62 ½, 1 day work threshing buckwheat .62 ½, help butcher hogs ½ day .50,

Value Kilson: help butcher 4 hogs .50, 1 day sowing pasture, 1 bush potatoes, 1 bush corn, 2 bush rye, 2 bush rye, 5 days work at hay 6.25, to 2.00, 6 lb veal, ½ bushel meal, 1 bushel corn, 4 days work getting hay 5.00, to 3.00, 2 bush rye, to cash to by lime 1.50.

Mary Jane Kilson: 7 yds fine cotton cloth, 1 yd muslin, 1 day absent .13, black silk mantle, velvet ribbon, Sept 1852 to cash 8.25.

Joseph Mauwee: draw corn stalks 1.00, to 50.00, paid Joseph Kilson 80.00 being the balance

1842-1852 Lorenzo & Morehouse Account Book

January 1843 **Jacob Mauwee**
Tabacco & Sunccue[?]

February 1843 **Truman Bradley**
6x9 glass, 6x8 glass, ¾ sheeting, box matches, 4 ---silk

June 1852 **Value Kilson**
Two days [labor?], 10 bush apples, sussbrim, hay 2 ½

November-December 1852 **Truman Bradley**
Picking apples, husking corn,

January- October 1853 **Truman Bradley**
Butchering, Paid for services, 15 bsh apples, cash paid by [demand?],
labor preformed (April- May),

June 1854 **Truman Bradley**
Purchase 192 ½ lbs beef, 2 bundles of straw.

1851-1860 Asa Slade Account Book

March 1854 **Value Kilson & Truman Bradley**
Paid cash to Kilson & Bradley, To cash for Value K

August 1853- July 1854 **Truman Bradley**
September: Codfish, coffee, tea, whip. November: 2 pairs shoes,
balance on corn, 10 pds. Codfish, 2 yds. Boilhed S---, 1 sheet of wadding.
November: By Cash
December: 1 gal Molasses, ½ pd. Tobacco, 3 oz. salt peter, I pkg
tobacco paper, to trade 11.00

March-July 1854 **Truman Bradley**
March: by cash
May: 4 pds. 10 oz. butter, 2 lbs. [?]
June: 1 shovel, 1 vest, 1 hat,
July: to trade, balance on hand 3.55
August 1859 Truman Bradley credit by baskets 1.30
-balance on shoes .17

October1853- April 1860 **Value Kilson**
October 1853: 1 [cap?]
June: 1 scythe
July: 6 yds [?] cloth
August: 1 gal molasses, ½ lb. tea, ½ lb. tabbaco
July: by cash 1.00

August: 1 oz. nutmeg, 3 [gal?] Vinegar

November 1854: Received of Value Kilson eight dollars which will balance book amounts if he has a receipt of 1.50.

March 1855: two pounds crackers, 1 bottle bitters, 1 pr. Boots, ¼ lb. snuff, by [---?] & cash 2.74

May: Tea & sugar

June: 1 hoe

October 1855 cash to balance 2.21.

December 1857: 1 lb. tobacco, 10 yds. Cloth

April 1858: 13 lbs nails, wife 10 yds of calico

November 1858: 2 pairs small boots/ 2 socks

July 1859: 10 yards of Calico 1.25

1860 Interest 2% year 4.99

1851 South Kent Furnace Ledger

February 1851 **Truman Bradley**

8 yards toweling

2 yards Calico

[?] & Tabacco

1 sack rye flower

Tabacco

1 set barn hinges

1 gal molasses

2 gal nails

Saw[?] [?]

1 corn basket

1 plug tobacco

By 4 1/2 days labor 75

February 1851 **Value Kilson**

1 sack white flour

1 Sali[r]tus

½ plug tobacco

3 ½ yds. Calico

1 cake soap

2 candles

5 lb. feed

1 sack [?] w flour

1 Sali[?]tus

½ plug tobacco

Ball an of [goods?]

By 4 ½ days labor 75
[2?] [to?] on mols
¼ snuff
February 1851 **George w. Bradley**
    To plate of Oysters
    To lot of Segares
    1 plate oysters
March 1851 **Value Kilson**
    1 pr shoes
    1 plug tabacco

March 1851 **George W. Bradley**
    ½ lb. Venision
    1 papers tobacco
    1 plate oysters
    1 ½ doz eggs
    2 plugs tobacco
    1 bot ink
    1 pen
    1 doz eggs
    To paid Mrs Baisly 1.00
    To 6 plugs tobacco
    To six plugs tabacco

March 1851 **Joseph Kilson**
    By the above turn with Ira Pudd on S C[?] matter
    To 7 yds Muslin
    To 1 pas [Book?]

April 1851 **Joseph Kilson**
    To Paid Ira Judd

April 1851 **Truman Bradley**
    30 yards Muslin
    4 spool thread

May 1851 **Truman Bradley**
    1 gal. Molasses
    1 lb. coffee
    To Ballc on goods .22

May 1851 **Joseph Kilson**
    5 yds Jean,
    buttons

May 1851 **Abel Beach**
To Paid Truman Bradley see his bill

June 1851 **Truman Bradley**
    To 1 ¼ Rope
    1 Boot box [?]
    1 box D[?]
    1 doz Buttons

June 1851 **Abel Beach**
    To 13 lb flour to Truman

July 1851 **Truman Bradley**
    To 1 carpet bag
    To [?] lickeshes
    1 lb of nails

July 1851 **Joseph Kilson**
    To pants & trimmings

August 1851 **Truman Bradley**
    To 2 pairs of shoes
    To 4 ready Made Bags
    To ½ - tobacco
    To ½ - tea
    To 1 pd Pepper
    To 2 boxes matches
    To 8 [Mackeral?]
    To 88 lbs feed
    To 1 pr boots
    To ½ -tabacco

September 1851 **Abel Beach**
1 axe Jo. Kilson

October 1851 **Truman Bradley**
    By P. Mitchell 1.00

October 1851 **Value Kilson**
     To qt Mackeral

October 1851 **Joseph Kilson**
     To 1 bot [?] Pectarae

November 1851 **Joseph Kilson**
     To cash 30
     By Henry [?] 30
     To 1 remnant cloth & heming
     To 1 comforter
     To 1 bot of Linimant
     To 1 yard toweling & hay
     By R. [?] 1.00

November 1851 **Truman Bradley**
     By Differences in exchange 10.00

December 1851 **Value Kilson**
     To 1 pr Reg Boots

1853 Account Book of Abel Beach Overseer.

Truman Bradley: help butcher beef .37 ½, 4 lb beef, ½ day trimming trees .31, 2 bush rye, 4 days work preparing for oats 2.50,

Joseph Mauwee: 6 ¼ lb veal, hoeing corn 3 ½ days 2.12, 4 ¾ days at cradling and securing grain 5.62, to cash 2.00, 26 ½ lb pork, 13 ½ lbs pork, 6 days work at corn 3.75, 5 lbs shortening, 2 bush wheat, by 1 day picking corn .62.

1854 Addendum to Account Book of Abel Beach.

Value Kilson: help butcher hogs .50, 2lbs veal, help butcher hogs cr, ½ bush potatoes, 23 lbs veal, ½ bush buckwheat, help butcher hogs .50, by work on school House 1.50.

Joseph Kilson: 2 bush wheat, 3 lb pork, 3 bush potatoes, 7 ¼ lbs veal, 9 lbs sole tether, 1 bush corn, keeping cow from Nov 3 1853 to May 1854 13.00, 2 lb veal, to cash 25.00, 6 ¾ lamb, 5 ½ lbs pork, to cash 5.00, 1 razor, to cash 15.00, 3 bush corn, 2 bush corn, ½ bush salt, to cash 10.00, 3 lb veal, 5 lb beef, 2 lb cotton wadding, 2 lb pork, 1 bushel potatoes, ½ bush potatoes, to cash 3.00, 1 barrel of flour, to cash 5.00, 2 bush potatoes, ½ bush potatoes,

Truman Bradley: help butcher hogs cr, by butchering hogs .50, one day cutting corn cr

Index

Note: ---- *indicates unknown last name. This index does not include the appendices.*

SCHAGHTICOKE MOUNTAIN, 68

SCHAGHTICOKE RESERVATION LANDS, Poorly Utilized 65 Rented out to Non-Indians 64 Sale of 65 67

SCHAGHTICOKE RESERVATION, 22 Lands Set aside for 42 Was within Mahican Tribal Territory 26

SCHAGHTICOKE TRIBAL NATION OF CONNECTICUT, vii 19-23 26 35 71 78 79

SCHAGHTICOKE TRIBE, so-called 60 78

SCHAGHTICOKE, Connecticut 28 34 a Place Name Not a People 60 Appearance of Moravian Community circa 1749 61 Became Dependent Upon State 64 67 Became Self-Reliant But Did Not Attain Political Autonomy 76 Burial Grounds 68 Decline of Moravian Community Population 48 Declining Population and Lack of Leadership 64 67 Economic Activity 74-76 Establishment 4 Indians There Were Not Considered Citizens of the Colony 56 Lack of Tribal Political Authority 71 Lacked Political Leadership 77 Lands Were Part of Mahican Territory 25 Marriage Rates 69 76 Mauwee First Associated With in 1741 33 Meaning of 3 Moravian Mission Ends 45 Not a Federally Recognized Tribe viii xi Political Authority 55 Political Community at 18

SCHAGHTICOKE, Connecticut (cont.) Presence of Political Leader circa 1743 17 18 Secularization 49 51 Settlement 7 Site of 3 24 Site Not Mentioned in Early Records 14 Social and Cultural Divisions 41 Transience 68 Two Distinct Communities 40 43 49 60 Unification of Population 55 59

SCHAGHTICOKE, New York 15 19 28 33 61

SECOND NEWTOWN PURCHASE, 16

SERGENT, John (Missionary at Stockbridge Indian Mission) 4 29 42

SHARMAN (SHERMAN), Daniel 51

SHARON, Connecticut 23 24 28 29 72 75 Schaghticoke Indians and Conflicts with Non-Christian Indian Groups 47

SHAWAS (ABRAHAM), (Mahican Indian) 25

SHECOMEKO (SHEKOMEKO), Mahican Village and Moravian Mission Site, 11 15 23 27 29 30 33 37 40 Some Villagers Migrated from New Milford 28

SHECOMEKO PETITION OF SHAWAS, 31

SHEFFIELD (WESTENHOOK), Massachusetts 3

SHERMAN, 51 Christian (Moravian Convert at Schaghticoke) 45 David 55 John 11 55 58 Peter 55 66 Petrus (Brother of Chere) 18 45 41 Roger (Colony Surveyor) 43

The Author

Mr. James P. Lynch is a nationally recognized ethno-historical research consultant. He has authored numerous research publications and articles on tribal land claims, tribal sovereignty and tribal history. His professional services are used by law firms, local, state and federal officials and agencies, and private sectors such as businesses, authors and network news media. Mr. Lynch is the owner of Connecticut-based Historical Consulting and Research Services. He can be contacted at jajpl@aol.com.

Made in the USA